AFFIRMATIONS
FOR EVERYDAY LIVING

AFFIRMATIONS
FOR EVERYDAY LIVING

Create More Clarity, Success,
and Joy in Your Daily Life

ANNIE ELIZABETH

River Sanctuary
PUBLISHING

Felton, California

Photography by Annie Elizabeth.*

Interior and cover design by DreamWriter (dreamwriterservices.com)

First edition January 2009
Second edition April 2010
Third printing January 2011

Printed in the USA

River Sanctuary Publishing
P.O. Box 1561
Felton, CA 95018
www.riversanctuarypublishing.com

Dedicated to the spiritual awakening of the New Earth

* **Many of the photographs in this book were taken on the uniquely beautiful grounds of *The River Sanctuary*.**

Acknowledgments

Thank you to my husband David for believing in me and mentoring the completion of this project. Thank you to Markos and Derek, my parents, my sister Barbara and her family (who are shown in several photos), and my friends and co-workers at Stanford University School of Medicine who inspired so much of my learning and growth.

Thank you to my editors Adra and Ardeth, my prayer partners for their love, and to my spiritual guides and teachers for their ever-present nurturing and patience.

Thank you to Chicho for staying by my side as long as he could.

To all spiritual travelers who have hungered, suffered, and searched for Truth… may you know lasting freedom and joy!

The River Sanctuary

CONTENTS

CHAPTER THREE: LIGHTING UP THE DARK PLACES

CHAPTER FOUR: EMPOWERING HEALTH AND VITALITY

CHAPTER FIVE: FLOWING AT HOME

CHAPTER SIX: HEALING YOUR RELATIONSHIPS

CHAPTER SEVEN: SHINING THROUGH THE BIG STUFF

Chapter Eight: Thriving at Work

Chapter Nine: Transcending Workplace Challenges

CHAPTER TEN: LIVING IN GRATITUDE

CHAPTER ELEVEN: EMBRACING YOUR PATH

Preface

The myriad situations, interactions, and experiences of daily life are an ideal laboratory for developing and practicing affirmative thinking. Affirmations support our arising awareness by helping us to break free of conditioned thought patterns that hold us back from the growth and expansion of consciousness that fulfills our deepest purpose as human beings.

The use of affirmations is not tied to any dogma or religious belief system. It is not necessary to believe in God or a Supreme Being to begin your practice with affirmations. Awareness of a Higher Power or Presence that exists within us and within all things arises naturally as we become free of our mental conditioning.

The use of affirmations supports us in moving toward greater happiness and personal power in our lives. On a more profound level, the practice of affirmations invokes Higher Power to partner with us even in our most mundane experiences.

The reward for paying attention to your thoughts is that you become more truly *present* in your immediate experience. You become an active participant in Creation by contributing the highest thought you are capable of having in each moment. Peering through the illusion of materiality, you begin to experience the world in an entirely new way. In those magical moments, the inherent beauty of life is restored and you get a taste of real freedom.

Now that you have embraced the awakening process, remember to be easy on yourself. Revel in each triumphant breakthrough, no matter how small or seemingly transitory. Though you will be blessed with sage guidance along the way, this is the ultimate personal quest. In your inner world, there is nothing to be attained, nothing to strive for or measure, and the destination is assured. There is no one ahead of you and no one behind you. The *journey* becomes the wellspring of your joy!

Introduction

The use of affirmations has been supported by spiritual masters and popularized in the self-help literature for many years as a technique for manifesting something we want to do, be, or have in our lives. Affirmations may be effectively used to:

- Maintain or restore optimal mental and physical health

- Create nurturing and sustaining relationships

- Resolve personal problems in work or family life

- Create a desired event or change in circumstances

- Improve prosperity and material well-being

- Experience a feeling of gratitude, inspiration, or fulfillment

- Invoke a blessing on behalf of someone else

Often employed along with *visualization*, practicing with affirmations can yield exciting and measurable results. Traditional *affirmations* and *denials* offered by great teachers and Masters are usually simple and direct statements targeted at shifting our thoughts in a direction that is more loving, confident, and joyful. We affirm what it is we want to have, or experience. We deny all possibility of doubt or resistance. The outcome that our life gets better is a direct result of the redirecting of our thinking about ourselves and our lives.[1]

Our daily life experiences provide an ideal laboratory for spiritual advancement. *Affirmations for Everyday Living* utilizes groups of related statements targeting common life situations, goals, and

challenges to stimulate your mind to let go of some of its many layers of conditioning and begin to function at a higher vibration. Along
with affirmations that can be used to improve your quality of life,

---

[1] Cady, Emilie. *Lessons in Truth.*

Affirmations for Everyday Living includes statements to help you
invite and become open to your Divine connection. Through this
process, you begin to free yourself of thinking that binds you to the
past and the future, heightening your ability to live in the Present
Moment, which is where ego evaporates and Spirit or God resides.

In using this book, be prepared for your mind to become uncomfortable or to react negatively to certain statements. Learn to pursue
your resistance, as it holds the key to uncovering your darkest places.
Construct new affirmations to address your deeper issues. As you
scan the titles or statements, thoughts or images of friends or family members will also come to mind. You experience joy through
the gift of service when you create affirmations on behalf of others.

When properly structured to stimulate a higher thought or break
your mind free from a limiting thought, an affirmation may bring
tremendous and seemingly miraculous results. In other cases, you
may hear yourself commenting that "my affirmation didn't work."
Or, more accurately, it didn't *appear* to work. Experiencing the
desired result depends upon your ability to recognize and do the
inner work necessary to prepare your mind to receive that which
you are requesting. When we are unaware of the thoughts that are
blocking us, our affirmations may seem ineffectual. More often,
what we desire has already taken form in the realm of Spirit, but
there is a delay in its appearance in the physical world.

It is my hope that what is contained in this book achieves a
balance of specialized situations with those that are universal in
human experience. That said, the selected chapters and topics
(situations, goals, or challenges) included in the book are best understood as illustrative rather than attempting to be definitive.

The chapters of *Affirmations for Everyday Living* present
groupings of affirmative statements addressing selected topics
(situations, goals, or challenges). Topics are organized within

chapters focusing on uplifting your mind, undoing negative think-ing, addressing toxic mental states, creating vibrant physical health, sustaining a happy home life, healing your relationships, handling major life events, feeling fulfilled in your work, negotiating work-place challenges, expressing gratitude, and walking the spiritual path.

You are invited to use the statements as they are, in any combination, or simplify, modify, extrapolate, or expand on them to meet a particular situation or desire. Commentary is provided in many cases to assist in understanding the context of the statements, as well as to provide a frame of reference for the approach taken.

Using affirmations does not require adopting any religion or belief system. On the contrary, the purpose of this practice is to restore your personal relationship with *Divine Love* that lives inside each one of us. You do not have to believe in anything or believe anything for affirmations to work. To begin, it may be fruitful to suspend an analytical approach and embrace "experimental faith." As the results of your affirmations are demonstrated in your expe-rience, your faith expands to become the foundation for your life.

In writing this book, a fundamental dilemma arose as to how to refer to the unfathomable phenomenon that is *God*, that which gives forth and sustains all life, to which (or to whom) our affirma-tions are directed. For many people, *God* is understood as a Supreme Being or a deep and all-accepting *Presence*, experienced with the same passionate feeling as that between a parent and a child. To others, *God* is understood and experienced as a neutral *Energy* that permeates within and throughout all Existence. As we continue to awaken, we come to accept that sometimes *God* will be experienced as a *Loving Presence* and at other times as *Essential Energy*.

The most commonly used reference in the book is *God*. Various other names are used, in accordance with what flowed through me at the time. I have taken poetic license in placing the names in italics with the first letter capitalized so as to identify and represent the holiness of this *Power*. Other words used in the affirmative state-ments that describe qualities of the *Divine Essence* are capitalized. I beg your indulgence of such idiosyncracies of my writing style.

Some of the many appellations for this *Supreme Being* or *Supreme*

Energy are presented on the following page. These are offered as examples, while at the same time acknowledging that the list does not begin to capture the magnitude of possibilities. Do not get attached to the Name. You are encouraged to modify the language in these affirmations to reflect your relationship with the *Master Energy Source*. Each of us expresses our conceptualization or terminology for *God* in a way that is harmonious with our character and life experience.

Affirmations for Everyday Living offers a practice using affirmations to implant new thoughts into your mind in response to common life situations, goals, and challenges. As you free yourself from conditioned thinking, you experience greater clarity, vitality, effectiveness, creativity, and joy. Through this process, the true creative power of your mind is restored.

Wherever you are on your path, my hope is that this book will stimulate your growing awareness and support you in each breakthrough. May your achievements in the outer world be an outpouring of your heart's greatest joy. May you bask in simpatico companionship with others who appreciate the adventure of this time of transition as much as you do. Let the arising of your new consciousness contribute to evolving the *Essence* that is *God*.

God is...

Supreme Being   Father

Unconditional Love   Truth

Infinite   Eternal

The Source of All That Is

Omnipotent   Omnipresent

Holiness (Wholeness)

Lord of All Creation

The Present Moment   The Silence

Our Essential Nature

Life-Force Energy   Pure BEING

Mother   Gaia/The Earth

Intelligence   The Master Mind

Oneness   Infinite Awareness

The Stillness   The Divine in Each of Us

All Knowing   All Seeing

The Zero Point Field   Pure Potentiality

Consciousness   Presence   NOW

All in All   Higher Power

Supreme Passion   Joy   Peace

Compassion   Our Highest Inner Voice

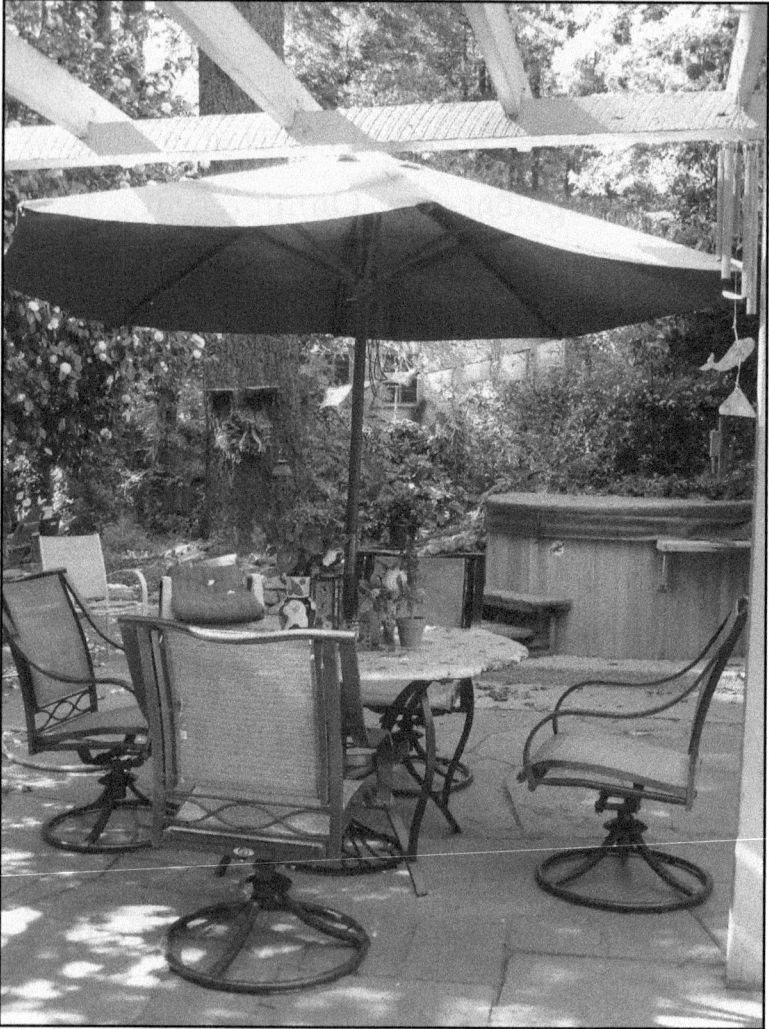

How Affirmations Work

In its simplest form, an affirmation is a positive statement of what you desire to be, have, do, or feel in a given moment, in the activities of your day, or in your life experience. An affirmation is most powerful when spoken aloud while in an attitude of prayer or "turning inward." Results are also generated when an affirmation is read or repeated silently. The power generated through an affirmation can be reactivated when recalling a statement that was spoken or read earlier in the day.

Many of the affirmations offered in this book are intended to effect changes in your thoughts or response to external conditions, thus bringing about corresponding changes in your life experience. Because our personal happiness is intrinsically linked to the happiness of family and friends, many of the affirmations are easily modified to assist those you love and wish to help. Affirmations can be directed toward any situation where you wish to affect change for the better.

Affirmations are positive prayer

In the *New Thought* movement, affirmations are referred to as positive prayer.[1] This is to distinguish this practice from the form of supplicating prayer, where an entreaty is made to a God that resides someplace outside of oneself, such as many of us were taught in our early religious training.

The power of positive prayer (affirmations) goes beyond mere positive thinking or "looking on the bright side." Affirmations are designed so as to state the outcome or result you are envisioning as if it had already occurred or been received in your life experience. Affirmations create a bridge from the physical (manifested) world to the domain of Pure Potentiality or the Unmanifested, activating the object or result of your desire so that it takes form in your life.[2] You do not need to concern yourself with how it will happen, or get caught up in the details. In fact, worrying about the details interferes with the process. You *know* that what you wish has already taken place, as you participate with delight in the unfolding.

Affirmations respond to the Law of Attraction

The use of affirmations is also referred to as *scientific prayer* because the results occur in accordance with principles (or *laws*) that are demonstrable in the physical world. For example, you may hold in mind a wish for help in planning a renovation project, and soon unexpected visitors arrive who coincidentally have these talents and happily share them. A negative thought attracts an outcome in the same way, such as a thought you are having "I hope he doesn't sit down next to me," and in the next instant, that's exactly what takes place. As you begin to pay attention to these *demonstrations* in your life, you become aware that you draw your experiences to you according to the thoughts you are holding in your mind.

It is said that "you get what you are thinking about, whether you want it or not." This has been referred to as the principle or Law of Attraction.[3] Your thoughts leave your mind in the form of energy, which communicates with the domain of Pure Potentiality. This realm is a place of neutrality, of nonjudgment, where your requests evoke a response in accordance with the focus or strength of your desire. The Law of Attraction reminds us that all thoughts are creative, emitting energy that is vibrating at a particular frequency, and that this energy attracts like unto itself.

Affirmations reprogram your thoughts

An affirmation can give strength to an idea or request that you are holding in your heart, thus accelerating your readiness for its arrival in your life. In other cases, affirmations serve to support your resolve when you are struggling with negative thoughts or mental states that seem to be taking you further from the goal. Affirmations have an effect even when your conscious mind feels unable to believe in, or to hold in certainty, the possibility of that which you seek to experience.

Subconscious destructive patterns of thought often underlie and infiltrate your responses to the day to day interactions and skirmishes of life. These negative thought patterns hold you back and retard your progress toward better experiences.

Today, you are joined by many companions as you walk the path to healing your mind and reclaiming your freedom as a creative being. Through conscious practice with affirmations, you choose to undertake the work of reprogramming your thoughts (your Subconscious mind). The direct result of reprogramming or positivizing your thoughts is to put you on a path toward greater effectiveness and fluidity —and receipt of Divine Grace — in your life.

Affirmations invoke power of the spoken word

Metaphysically speaking, the power of affirmations is based in large part on the augmentation of energy that occurs when a thought is given power through the spoken word. Affirmations permeate the Subconscious mind, which in turn automatically influences the Conscious mind:

> *Infinite potencies of sound derive from the creative word. Any word spoken with clear realization and deep concentration has a materializing value. Words saturated with sincerity, conviction, faith, and intuition are like highly explosive vibration bombs, which, when set off, shatter the rocks of difficulties and create the change desired.*[4]

All uses of the voice, such as singing and chanting, add strength to your practice of affirmations.

Affirmations invoke a response outside of time

According to new understandings and dialog around quantum physics, sequential time is merely a convenience to slow things down and create order in our experience on this plane of existence. Current explorations remind us that we are beings composed of, and operating through, laws of energy rather than materiality (the manner in which we have agreed to define our world, at least in the West).

In this sense, all feelings or states of being exist simultaneously in the realm of Pure Potentiality. This is also conveniently referred to as *The Field*.[5] All potential thoughts and all potential experiences exist simultaneously in the Field, and what you are doing is selectively calling forth experience according to your ability — according to the level of your consciousness. Because your level of consciousness is capable of infinite expansion, your potential for experiencing or manifesting what you desire is unlimited.

These new realizations have brought many of us to understand that we are Eternal beings, connected with a Field of energy that flows in and through all things, including us. As you progress in this understanding, you come to know that your essential nature is one of happiness and joy. Your fundamental goal is to move toward increasing receptiveness of a positive feeling or experience of being.[6]

When you affirm something, you are calling forth a response from the Field, in alignment with the vibration of your desire, to be manifested in the world of your experience.

Outcomes result from interaction of energy

You are beginning to understand and experience that the essence of *Who You Really Are* is not contained in or limited to a physical body. Your physical body is nothing more or less than a container for your true self, which at its most basic is an embodiment of Divine Energy seeking experiences that allow you the memory of your origin and true nature.

The baseline teaching of what is known as New Thought can be summarized as *You Create Your World Through Your Thoughts*. At the same time, you do not have singular control over the outcome of a situation. You are a being comprised of and emitting energy that is enmeshed and interwoven with the energy of all the beings with whom you are interacting. This enmeshment produces an outcome in any situation that is an expression of the complex web of energies (thoughts) that created it.

As such, any given experience may not appear to be exactly what it was you thought you were asking for — and indeed, it is not. It is in this sense that New Thought teaches that We Are All One. That is because our life energies are not separate, but are interacting in a constant commingling to produce experiences and outcomes.

The results you receive from your affirmations are thus dependent upon the complexity of the energy around the request. Your goal is to accept whatever happens and reflect on the ways in which it serves your good, knowing that the outcome always addresses the Highest Good of all whose energy is invested in the situation.

What about negative or hurtful thoughts that another person may be sending into the universe to work against you? What about the negative thoughts you see drifting across your own mind? We find comfort in knowing that the power of a positive thought is many times that of a negative thought. In addition, outcomes that appear on the surface to be negative are in fact valuable learning experiences pointing out areas where subconscious limiting thoughts are embedded in your mind. You then become better able to target these thoughts for healing and transcendence.

Affirmations invoke Good or God in your life

At the root of all action or desire is the basic principle of choice, whether to move toward Good, or God, toward the Light — or away from Good, toward the darkness, toward chaos and fragmentation. Affirmations open a channel for Supreme Energy to flow into your life. Underlying the affirmations is the awareness of a great and expansive Energy Source that sustains all life, to which (or to whom) your affirmations are directed. A basic tenet of New Thought is that *God* cannot be defined and does not exist separately from your individual perception of Him/Her/It. As your awareness deepens, your understanding and experience of *God* deepens — and that expansion continues forever and ever.

Affirmations and Forgiveness

Forgiveness is a process that enables you to move forward in the evolution of your soul toward greater wholeness (holiness) and connection with *All That Is*. Through forgiveness, you experience a deeper level of reverence and appreciation toward yourself and your world. An attitude of openness and trust borne of forgiveness underlies many of the affirmations in this book.

Forgiveness is a fundamental tenet of most major religious and spiritual practices. Wonderful books have been written and techniques offered to assist us in breaking through the obstacles to let go of painful memories of the past. Forgiveness in its broadest sense is the goal of most psychotherapeutic modalities. The psychological shift of forgiveness is the key to undoing the habitual chain of negative thoughts that gives rise to a patterned response to events and situations in our lives. Entrapment in these patterned responses is what holds us back from experiencing a new level of freedom.

Affirmations are a useful approach to an immediate experience of resentment or anger toward another (for example, a colleague who embarrassed you in a meeting, or your mother-in-law's hurtful remark). Employing affirmations is most effective when you catch yourself in a reactive thought immediately as it arises, isolating the thought, then creating an affirmation to counter it.

While the cause of an unloving thought may seem clear on the surface — as in "he did *this* to me" — the *true* cause of the emotion is rooted in a chain of wrong thinking. You take a step toward a deeper process of forgiveness by creating an affirmation that releases the other person of responsibility for your reaction.

Beyond the ability to speak the words "I forgive him," forgiveness involves undoing the thoughts underlying the belief that anyone other than yourself can be responsible for what you think and feel.

Over time, repetition of negative experiences with a person

confirms the opinion that you have of them, transforming resentments into a deeply held conviction or grudge. A grudge becomes a belief programmed in your psyche, in the same way that a traumatic event or painful experience may be imprinted on your soul memory.

While affirmative statements alone may not be effective in undoing deeply held beliefs about people or the effects of past trauma or pain in our lives, affirmations create an opening for the forgiveness process to arise in us. Affirmations invoke a shift in the energy around a negative situation or memory. This creates an avenue for a change in thinking to occur — that is, an undoing of the way in which a memory or thought is stored in our minds and the resultant chain of thinking that arises from it. Such a shift in perception is a *miracle*.[7]

A powerful method for engaging in a deeper experience of forgiveness can be found in an internal process known as *The Work*. Exercises such as the "Judge Your Neighbor Worksheet," and the "Turning it Around" that follows, open us to the discovery that resentment, criticism, and judgment of others brings us full circle to face our deepest judgmental thoughts about ourselves.[8]

Forgiveness is a practice involving a fearless intention to uncover the layers and work through the web of painful thoughts stored deep within your subconscious mind. As you work through each feeling or thought that arises, you learn that the process of forgiving others inevitably brings you back to forgiving yourself. You come to recognize the role your own thoughts played in inviting the situation, or at the very least in allowing the situation or event to occur through a lack of awareness.

In moving through the forgiveness process, you go beyond the pain and embrace every experience as a step in your learning. You then move on, knowing you have acquired new skills, making you capable of creating better and more fulfilling experiences. As you shed the burden of your past painful memories, you discover and come to identify with the Eternal "I" that exists beyond your Story.[9] You begin to incorporate forgiveness as a way of thinking and behaving in the world. More than being an action or activity, forgiveness becomes an approach to life in each moment. It is then that you discover what true freedom really means.

[1] Morrissey, Mary Manin. *New Thought: A Practical Spirituality.*
[2] Chopra, Deepak. *The Seven Spiritual Laws of Success.*
[3] Dyer, Wayne. *The Power of Intention.*
[4] Yogananda, Parmahansa. *Where There is Light.*
[5] McTaggart, Lynn. *The Field.*
[6] Hicks, Esther and Jerry. *The Amazing Power of Deliberate Intent.*
[7] Foundation for Inner Peace. *A Course in Miracles,* see also M. Williamson, *A Return to Love.*
[8] Katie, Byron. *Loving What Is.*
[9] Tolle, Eckhart. *A New Earth.*

Suggestions for Using This Book

Technique One. Tuning into the Silence

1. As you turn inward into silence for five minutes in the morning, or at any time during the day, observe your state of mind (your thoughts) and the feelings that are present in your body.

2. Ask yourself the following questions and target what you would like to focus on by watching for thoughts or feelings that arise:

    What would I like to be, do, or have more of in my life today?

    What thoughts are causing me physical, emotional, or mental distress as I imagine how my day will go? (or, if it is evening, as I look back on how my day went...)

    What am I feeling or thinking at this moment toward or on behalf of myself or another person that causes me to be unsettled or agitated?

3. When you have targeted a goal for the day, or a disturbing thought or feeling you'd like to work on, use the table of contents to locate a chapter and affirmation theme that most closely matches the goal, concern, or challenge.

4. Read through the entire set of statements. Select two or three statements that most closely fit your situation, or that resonate somehow within you. Often these are the statements that produce a feeling of resistance within us.

5. Modify the language of your chosen statements as needed to make them more specific to your situation or goals.

6. Speak each statement, first loudly, then softly and more slowly. Do this several times. Combine with visualization of an outcome or a scenario if this works for you.

7. Turn inward and reflect on the words or ideas presented in the affirmation for two or three minutes. See what comes up for you. Journal your thoughts, observe them, and allow your learning to unfold.

8. Move into a state of deep concentration on the meaning contained in the words. Jot down your favorite statements on a sheet of paper to carry with you during the day. Read and repeat the statements out loud at two other points during the day.

9. It is also powerful to engage in this practice in the evening, perhaps addressing something that has come up for you during the day.

Technique Two. Affirmations as Part of Prayer Treatment

Affirmations may be embedded in Prayer Treatment (see Chapter Five interlude *Learning to Work with Infinite Power*, p. 85).

Technique Three. Opening the Book at Random

Sit quietly and invite Spirit to lead you to a set of statements that has meaning for your practice today. Allow your hands to be guided to select a page. Experience the statements contained on a page as you open your mind to the special message that is waiting there just for you.

Technique Four. Repeating Affirmations before Sleeping

Repeating an affirmation as you are getting ready to sleep can be powerful. Combine with visualization to strengthen your request.

Technique Five. Affirmations on Behalf of Other People

Follow steps three through six to select an affirmation that will bring improvement or healing to a friend or family member. Speak the affirmation aloud using the person's name.

CHAPTER ONE

CULTIVATING A HEALTHY MIND

The thought might then come, "I don't have to imitate anybody else." With this thought you might begin to feel free of other people's opinions about you. From this, a desire arises to act with integrity, to show the world that you know who you are. Thus, from one tiny sensation a whole new pattern emerges; you have found the path of expanded awareness.

Deepak Chopra, *Book of Secrets*

Interlude

Using Affirmations to Improve
Your Thoughts

The affirmations in the first three chapters are directed toward improving your ability to consciously direct your mind and your thoughts. The first chapter provides clusters of affirmative statements that reinforce positive thoughts and nurture healthy attitudes.

Affirmations in Chapter Two focus on challenging thoughts and attitudes that are common in response to certain general life situations or occurrences. Chapter Three invites you to explore your mind to unravel some fear-derived mental states. You might question whether the use of affirmative statements can really turn around deeply ingrained habits of mind. It's not as if affirmations are a panacea for everything that is not perfect about us. As is the case with exercising to lose weight, or getting massage therapy to relieve carpal tunnel syndrome, the return to wellness is a process that requires some degree of self-discipline and application over time. Affirmations are a tool for such a purpose. Over time, results are assured.

The use of an affirmation triggers your mind to have a new thought. Given the intense thought conditioning that comprises who you have come to believe you are, the invitation to have a different thought refreshes your mind and wakes it up, if only temporarily. The affirmation invites your mind to travel along a new line of thinking, which it actually finds exciting and exhilarating — that is, until the new thought butts up against something that threatens the ego's comfortable position of authority. So, expect your affirmations to stir things up for you. If you feel upset, that's an invitation to explore more deeply inside your mind for what is causing the disturbance.

When you react to an experience or a thought you are having, your mental state produces energy that attracts more thoughts and consequently more experiences of a similar energy vibration or frequency. That is, negative thoughts attract negative experiences; positive thoughts attract positive experiences. Affirmations support you in responding to your experiences in a way that allows you to move to a level of better feeling or a more positive energy vibration. Over time, you retrain your mind to choose this better feeling rather than continually being drawn into drama and unhappiness.

Through the use of affirmations, we become more able to recognize and undo destructive or harmful thoughts. Affirmations create a more positive interpretation and response to our world, thereby increasing our experience of contentment, peace and joy.

Everyday Affirmations

Every day my understanding of
God as *the Source of All That Is*
grows stronger and deeper.

* * * * * *

Every day I contribute to the lives of others in meaningful
ways. I am valued for what I do.

* * * * * *

Every day brings me experiences of Calm,
Contentment, Love, and Joy.

* * * * * *

I am invigorated with boundless Energy,
Confidence,
a sense of Purpose and Fulfillment,
as I create the incredible hours, days, and years
of this lifetime.

* * * * * *

Every day I fall more deeply in Love with Life.

*These affirmations are empowering when spoken at the beginning of the day.
Used individually or in combination, these statements set your intention
to experience what is most alive in you as the adventure of each new day
unfolds.*

Welcoming More Good into Your Life

Knowing that the Universe is only Good waiting to be called
forth, I open NOW to receiving Good
in all domains of my Life.

* * * * * * *

My good fortune is the outpouring of the Universe in
response to my desire for wellbeing.

* * * * * * *

Welcoming my Good allows those around me
to receive more Good in their lives.

* * * * * * *

My Good is a demonstration of the Divine Gift of Grace that
is available to all souls in Creation.

Have you ever held back from creating outlandish wealth or beauty for yourself because you think it means someone else in the world is going to be deprived of it or suffer as a result? Because the nature of the Universe is Infinite Supply, embracing your Good cannot deprive others from attracting to themselves what it is they desire. In fact, the reverse is true. The Abundance that you invite to yourself is a message to others encouraging them to create their own Prosperity and Joy. As you retrain your mind to know that Good is the only Reality, you begin to experience Grace. Grace means that good things come to you the more you open to that Reality, not necessarily because you have earned it or deserve it. Grace Happens!

Feeling Safe in the World

My mind is at perfect peace today.

* * * * * * *

I am capable of handling all experiences of life.

* * * * * * *

Thoughts or imaginings of future pain or loss
cannot disturb my peace.

* * * * * * *

All is well in my world NOW.
Every thought I have affirms this.

~~~~~~

*My husband rarely struggles with thoughts of vulnerability or not feeling
safe in the world. But for me it is as if a deep insecurity and sense of
impending doom is imprinted on my soul.*
*All fear-based thoughts are a product of the egoic self and are not real.[1] As
you begin to reprogram your thoughts toward the One Reality — which
is Love — your experience of the world changes. As you change your
thoughts about what you experience, your world becomes a loving place
because YOU are loving. This is the essential Truth that is awakening in
our world today.*

---

[1] Williamson, Marianne. *A Return to Love.*

Believing in Yourself — Going for Your Highest Dream

I am unlimited in who I can be
or what I can accomplish in this lifetime.

* * * * * *

I live in the NOW in which everything is possible.

* * * * * *

The steps to accomplish my dream are made clear to me
in Divine timing.

* * * * * *

I bless and release old ideas of parents, friends,
or other family members about what I can do
or who I should be.

* * * * * *

The perfect outcome is already accomplished.

When you take the greatest dream you have for yourself and project it into the future, you may find yourself plagued by doubt or disbelief. Our mental chatter tells us, "You'll never be able to have that... do that... be that" person you feel you are deep inside. This feeling of inadequacy may be reinforced by less than positive reactions and comments of others with whom you share your dream. In the formative stages of your visioning, speak about your dream only to those who will bless and honor your intention, rather than fixating on the details.

Living in the Present Moment

I Am Present to Life in This Moment.

* * * * * * *

I let go of meaningless details of the past
which occupy space in my mind.

* * * * * * *

I Am Open to the experience of
something greater than the story that is ME.

* * * * * * *

I embrace What Is Real and experience
true Freedom in the NOW.

The egoic mind derives its sense of Self or identity from memory of past experiences. Your mind is programmed to habitually project concepts derived from the past to define the present moment. New realms of experience open as you learn to recognize and move beyond this habitual thought pattern to discover your "true self," which exists only in the Present Moment.

Awakening Empathy and Compassion (commentary)

How easy it is to open our hearts to those we see in news stories experiencing tragedies somewhere far across the globe! The best laboratory for developing true compassion is the everyday interactions we have with others in our daily life.

Be alert to your mind drawing sweeping conclusions (whether silently or aloud), "he is such a troubled person ..." "she should think about...."
Feelings of discomfort, closing your heart, or feeling there is something that the other person needs to change, all point to matching energies in your own experience, whether in this lifetime or another. In opening to these feelings, you experience another person's path as your own. You free yourself of any residual energy or mental reaction that limits you.

Every encounter is an opportunity to become more adept at seeing through the ego that is presenting in another. We learn to greet the Divine Soul housed within that person, and the other person sees the Divine Soul that is in us.

Awakening Empathy and Compassion

I experience Empathy and Compassion in my life today.

* * * * * *

There is no life condition or personal choice that is strange
to me or that I must invalidate.

* * * * * *

All life conditions (choices) are steps on the path
to knowing God. I honor every story as my own.

* * * * * *

All who are brought into my sphere are deserving of
my attention and care. I open to inner guidance on my role
and correct action in every situation.

* * * * * *

As I open my heart in Nonjudgmental Love,
I communicate Healing and Compassion.

* * * * * *

As I offer Compassion, I receive Compassion.
I release and am Free of all memories or resonating
frequencies to this story that reside in my Soul.

Developing Personal Power

The best outcome for the family, group, or organization is
also the best outcome for me.

* * * * * * *

My thoughts seek that which furthers the
Highest Good for all involved in
every situation or project.

* * * * * * *

I am a source of strength, wellbeing, companionship,
and growth to those who seek to partner with me.

* * * * * * *

I cease defining myself according to my job or my role.
I offer my talents in service of the Good
of the Whole.

When you use your position in the organization or group to override others and bring about something that furthers yourself, you are operating in Force mode. When you hold the good of the group as your intention, your Personal Power influences the outcome. *Recent research shows that the vibratory frequency of thoughts motivated by the good of the whole is significantly higher than that of more self-centered, ego-based thoughts.[1] In this way, an apparently insignificant individual can wield tremendous power.*

---

[1]Hawkins, David R, *Power Versus Force.*

Living in Joy

I accept JOY as the only thought, the only meaning, the only reaction to *All That Is.*

* * * * * * *

The brightness of the Light that is Life
shines in my Being for all to see.

~~~~~~~~~~~~~~~~~~~~~~~~~~~~~~~

Happiness occurs in response to something, such as when you have a good day, receive a compliment, or are remembered by a friend. Joy is different from happiness in that it is a state of wellbeing or high frequency vibration that is not in response to anything or dependent on anything. Joy is a place in the mind that is Acceptance, beyond judgment. In this sense Joy and Love are similar, with Love being an all-encompassing Joy that reaches out to embrace the entire Universe. For many of us, Joy is experienced in brief flashes of transitory awareness — something we wish and hope to experience more of as we progress on our path. Along the way, our experience of Joy deepens as we affirm what we know to be true. When I am mindful, I endeavor to project joy and kindness to every person I encounter during the day. I am struck by the wonderful smiles and acts of kindness I witness everywhere, from the student to the secretary to the salesperson. And then at other times, I am aware of a deep darkness that floats beneath the surface of my thoughts, as if my joy is merely a veneer on the desolation that is lurking below. This is the awareness of the human condition that we all carry. In this simple statement, we affirm our experience of something beyond the transitoriness of human suffering.

Creating Your Personal Vision

I AM . . .

CAPABLE   ENCHANTING

AGELESS   KIND   GENTLE

HUMBLE   POWERFUL

VIGOROUS   ENERGETIC

COMPASSIONATE   PROSPEROUS

INTELLIGENT

CLEAR-THINKING

ALIGNED WITH TRUTH

CONFIDENT

LOVED BY GOD

In the early years of my job, it was routine for me to suffer feelings of insecurity and dread when I attended large conferences. I created this affirmation in the hotel room one year and repeated it over and over as I swam in a marvelous historic pool that had a view of the sky through a glass ceiling. The effect was dramatic and immediate; I had a great time at the meeting, and all subsequent meetings. Create your own version by substituting words and phrases that rise to your mind when you are quietly sitting.

CHAPTER TWO

ELEVATING YOUR ATTITUDES

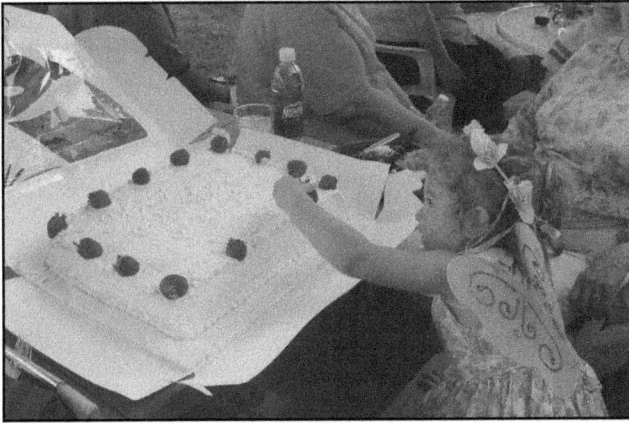

You relate to everything and everyone on this planet through the mechanism of thought. It is not what is in the world that determines the quality of your life, it is how you choose to process your world in your thoughts.

Wayne Dyer, *You'll See It When You Believe It*

Interlude

Don't Worry, Be Happy

The words to this well-known song (written and sung by Bobby McFerrin) carry a deep message. For many in our culture, "worry-mode" has become the predominant State of Being, and is perceived to be normal and even comfortable.

But isn't worry is a good thing? you ask. Worrying reminds me to take care of things I need to do. When you worry about something coming up for yourself, like a job interview, it's a way of reminding yourself to look ahead and plan. The Boy Scout motto *"Be Prepared"* is valuable in teaching kids to think ahead and plan for contingencies, such as, to pack for cold weather when heading into the mountains. This is a good thing. So when does planning cross the line to become worry? It crosses the line when you can't turn off that tape running in your head. (You may find yourself using a bit of alcohol or marijuana to abate that chatter for a time.) When needing to plan, we affirm that all the details come together with a minimum of fuss. We take positive action at the right time, and then we let it go.

"Well, I don't worry about myself," you might say, "I only worry about other people. It's my way of showing I care." Worry, labeled in a more friendly way as "concern," is one of the favorite tools of the ego to keep you in a *thinking* rather than a *being* mode. You may have learned how not to overtly meddle in the affairs of others, but the mind finds it almost irresistible to ponder on someone else's situation. We feel important when we are solving another person's problems in our head. It boosts our ego to think we know better.

In fact, on a spiritual and energetic level, worry is not an expression of caring, but an expression of doubt in that person's ability to create the next steps they need for their learning. Such thoughts actually reinforce a negative belief we hold about that person, or they may hold about themselves. I may worry about my son taking the steps to find a better job because "he always procrastinates." In this case, I am projecting my son's past behavior into the future and not allowing him the possibility of growth. He may not choose to take his next step when I think he needs to, but it's *his* next step, not mine. On the other hand, if I am concerned about having to continue helping him pay his rent, then I have a need of my own wrapped up in the outcome that has to be addressed. In this case, I make sure I communicate my concerns to my son. I affirm a positive outcome in the situation, trusting that the Highest Good for all will be served.

Why should you be worried about worry? The mental activity of worry sends a signal to your endocrine system to prepare for an attack, to send adrenaline into your bloodstream just as if you were a performer waiting to be called to the stage at any moment. When you are in worry mode, you are "on," you are geared up, you feel you are ready for anything. That is the predominant mode of being for many people in our society today, and we give and receive lots of approval to one another for that.

But, isn't it good to be "ready for anything?" As taught so well in Buddhism, it's a question of balance. Chronic worry becomes anxiety, which is an unconscious steady state of wariness and hyper-vigilance. The effect this has on your body is that blood is channeled to the bones and muscles and away from the processes going on in the major organs. In this state, your cells do not properly rest and replenish themselves, with disease as the long term result.

When your thoughts are engaged in worry, you are not in Present Time, which is where the experience of true happiness lies. So, don't worry, be happy!

Self-Esteem — Remembering Your True Nature

I Am a part of *Source Energy*.
I am loved unconditionally and beyond measure.

* * * * * *

I do not have to ACHIEVE anything, or BE anything,
for my Life to have Meaning.

* * * * * *

I do not have to be PERFECT
for my Life to have Value.

* * * * * *

I let go of all thoughts and attitudes that
diminish myself or others.

* * * * * *

I receive from within me
the Truth of Who I Really Am.[1]

Our egoic self sends us messages that confirm a deep-seated belief that we are buffoons, failures, crazy — that we just don't measure up on one level or another. We unwittingly reinforce this by assessing each person we meet using the same harsh standards. Nonjudgment is the key to our freedom.

---

[1] Foundation for Inner Peace. *A Course in Miracles.*

Allowing Others to Make Mistakes — Letting Go of Worry

I take delight in allowing [person] to create her experiences
and next steps for learning in her own way.

* * * * * * *

I know that [person's] lessons and path are unique
and that he is equipped to make perfect decisions
for his learning.

* * * * * * *

My worry thoughts are transformed into a
positive statement of blessing for [person].
I see her path surrounded by Light.

* * * * * * *

I acknowledge my own needs and desires, and ask that the
Highest Good be manifested for all concerned.
I receive direction on any action to take in accordance with
my desire to help [person].

~~~~~~~~~~~~~~~~~~~~~~~~~~~~~~~~~

*We all know "we learn by making mistakes," but it is hard not to meddle
in the affairs of others when you think you know better! Here you invite
your mind to transform worry thoughts into positive statements of blessing
for the path of a person. Keeping a journal and writing down the blessings
you create is powerful in undoing worry thoughts. You also invite your
Right Action in the situation.*

Abundance — Having What You Desire

Abundance pours from an Infinite Fountain
into the vessel of my Life.

* * * * * *

I KNOW that everything I desire is already given.
All that I need to do is receive it.

* * * * * *

I am free of all thoughts and energies that sabotage
my receiving my Good.

* * * * * *

In opening to my Abundance, I open to the
Abundance of all people.

* * * * * *

I am healed, I deserve, I forgive, I receive.
I extend my blessing to others.

*We go inside and dig out the root thoughts that keep us trapped in lack
and limitation. We courageously work through our self-loathing and our
victimhood, taking heart as each breakthrough is followed by a deeper
dimension of challenge. All are blessed in this process.*

Nonjudgment — Cultivating Loving-Kindness

I offer that part of my self that finds fault
with others to the *Holy Spirit* for healing.

* * * * * * *

I am free from the belief I must judge another,
or that another would judge me.

* * * * * * *

I am Free from the pain of judging another,
which is the same as judging Myself.

* * * * * * *

Love reaches through me to bless every person who enters
my thoughts,
restoring wholeness (Holiness) to All.

Because our True Selves consist only of Divine Substance, we ultimately come to know that We Are All ONE. The apparent separation between us is an illusion arising from our identification with bodies. You begin to see, on an energetic level, the ways in which the experience of another is also happening to you. Every judgment or "attack thought" against another is a condemnation of yourself, fueling your own deep sense of unworthiness and also feeding your Pain Body. The remedy is Atonement (At-One-Ment), or undoing of this habitual thought pattern, which is a gift of Divine Grace.

Self-Satisfaction — Believing You Accomplish Enough

I make perfect choices about when to work
and when to rest.

* * * * * * *

I am free of harsh judgments against myself
that diminish my sense of accomplishment
and weaken my resolve.

* * * * * * *

I delegate [these tasks] to *Divine Power* for assistance.

* * * * * * *

I am free of pressure and panic.
I am relaxed and in the flow.

* * * * * * *

All falls into place in the Right Way at the Right Time.

Along with thoughts focused on limitation and lack, or dependence on the approval of others, equally insidious is the gnawing sense that there is something else or something more you should be doing in order to give yourself that gold star you so long for. Or, sometimes you perceive that another person believes you are not doing something you should be doing. Bottom line: when you are in touch with your needs, you will always be doing exactly what it is you should be doing, and the outcome of your efforts is always perfect just the way it is.

Empowering Yourself — Breaking Free of Old Wounds
(commentary)

~~~~~~~~~~~~~~~~~~~~~~~~~~~~~~~~~~~~

There are many of us who are stuck in a habit pattern that maintains us in identification with a painful incident, illness, or occurrence of the past. Triggering the memory of old wounds feeds our Pain Body and is a significant factor in illness that does not heal.[1]

The continued search for an explanation must be seen for what it is — a means of keeping the incident alive in us. We are unable to own our energy in the moment and proceed in our lives as a genuine person who is Present as long as we hold on to the "dreadful story" as part of our self-definition.

---

[1] Myss, Caroline. *Why People Don't Heal, and How They Can*

Empowering Yourself — Breaking Free of Old Wounds

My experience of [bad experience] does NOT limit me
in any way from having the Good that is mine
in this lifetime.

* * * * * * *

I let go of the need to seek explanations
for why this experience happened to me.

* * * * * * *

I Am SPECIAL and important even after I let go
of this experience.

* * * * * * *

I gratefully welcome and receive all the lessons of this
experience. Karmic aspects surrounding this experience
are NOW complete.

* * * * * * *

All memory of this experience is released from my mind and
no longer conditions my idea of Who I Am.

* * * * * * *

I move on to the next step in my journey
with joyful anticipation.

Accepting Responsibility — Getting Beyond Blame — Forgiveness (commentary)

When Ego is in charge, your thoughts flip between blaming yourself to blaming someone else for a situation your mind labels as negative. Most of the time, your involvement in a bad or wrong situation comes from your having acted, or made yourself vulnerable to someone else's action, out of a wrong belief about the world. The negative experience is an opportunity to bring that wrong thought into your awareness to critically examine it, and thereby undo your negative programming.

Accepting Responsibility — Getting Beyond Blame — Forgiveness

I acknowledge my role in creating
[this situation or condition].

* * * * * * *

I am open to receiving the message from this experience that
helps me grow.

* * * * * * *

My motives in this situation are revealed to me. I invite
undoing of any thinking that is not aligned with
My Highest Good or the Highest Good of another.

* * * * * * *

I ask Forgiveness from those I may have harmed through
my lack of Understanding.

* * * * * * *

I forgive those who I perceive to have harmed me.
I forgive myself for not knowing enough to
avoid this mistake.

* * * * * * *

I give thanks and let go.

Accepting What Is — Breaking Through Resistance
(commentary)

~~~~~~

A feeling of anxiety evidenced by tightness in the solar plexus is a sure sign you are in resistance to your immediate circumstances or experience. In any new or challenging situation, your egoic self attempts to interpret and label the experience according to a match it pulls from your repertoire of the past. But when faced with genuine experience in the NOW, the egoic mind has nothing to offer and thus triggers an anxiety signal in your mind. You learn to respond by first accepting What Is, and then Trusting in your ability to know what to do next without having a clear roadmap. What was internally perceived as resistance or fear is then transmuted into openness and readiness to respond.[1] Over time, it becomes less important to analyze or make sense of a situation. As you grow in your practice, you gain more freedom from the egoic mind that needs to "figure things out." You open to receiving direction from a higher place inside you.

---

[1] Katie, Byron. *Loving What Is.*

Accepting What Is — Breaking through Resistance

Although I may not understand the situation
in which I find myself or the feelings I am experiencing,
I accept the conditions in which I find myself
as That Which IS.

* * * * * * *

I let go of inner resistance to the appearance
of my current situation.
I Trust that all my life experiences serve
my *Best and Highest Good*.

* * * * * * *

I Am guided in appropriate Thought, Word, and Deed.
I engage in Right Action, knowing that
all will be understood in the Right and Perfect Time.

Learning from Resentment or Anger

My own thoughts and not [person or situation] are the
cause of this feeling of resentment.

* * * * * * *

I NOW embrace new thoughts or attitudes that improve my
experience of [person or situation].

* * * * * * *

The loving Acceptance of *All That Is* encircles the negative
energy output of my thoughts, channeling them into the
Earth for healing.

* * * * * * *

I give thanks and bless [person or situation] for
bringing me an opportunity to grow and
become more self-aware.

---

*Experiences that trigger resentment can be as simple as someone cutting
you off in traffic, a child getting into trouble again, or an insensitive remark
from a friend or family member. Recognizing and releasing your feelings
and thoughts around this brings an immediate experience of relief. Anger
indicates a deeper issue that invites more exploration to uncover and work
through a need within you that is not being met.*[1]

---

[1] Rosenberg, Marshall. *Nonviolent Communication.*

Sanctifying Grief for the World

I cradle my feelings of Grief for those in the world
experiencing [sad event].

* * * * * * *

I sing with the angels a song of mourning that
has been sung since the beginning of Time.

* * * * * * *

I release these feelings to the healing
of *Universal Love*, and go forward in Joy,
knowing that the work I do
contributes to an end to sorrow for all time.

~~~~~~

And So It Is.
It may happen that you are accused of turning your back on evil and grief
in our world when you walk the path that heals your mind. This is not the
case. If anything, your sensitivity to human misery is heightened as your
awareness expands and you learn to be Present in your experience. But
you become aware that, when you share in thoughts or verbalizations of
despair and grief, you are contributing some of your life force energy (and
therefore giving life) to that which you abhor.[1]

---

[1] Foundation for Inner Peace. *A Course in Miracles*

CHAPTER THREE

LIGHTING UP THE DARK PLACES

Our deepest fear is not that we are inadequate. Our deepest fear is that we are powerful beyond measure. It is our light, not our darkness, that most frightens us. ... You are a child of God.
We are all meant to shine, as children do. And as we let our own light shine, we unconsciously give other people permission to do the same. As we're liberated from our own fear, our presence automatically liberates others.

Marianne Williamson, *A Return to Love*

Interlude

Making Friends with Your Pain Body

Here you take a step deeper into the workings of the mind to address conditioned habitual thought patterns, or states of mind. You are working here with thoughts that are so deeply ingrained in the unconscious part of your mind that they now constitute your orientation to life, your world view.

The fear, terror, and dread that appear to exist in the world — outside of ourselves — has expressed itself in myriad forms of violence in our shared history, and is exalted in our art forms and entertainment. This apparent reality, to which we see ourselves as subject, is a manifestation of the Collective Unconsciousness, or Pain Body, to which most of us are still connected and to which we have contributed in some fashion. "But that is not me! I'm not like that, I'm a good person," you are quick to say in defense of yourself. And we are, in our essential State of Being, all good people. The exercises in this section help return you to that state of belief in your essential wellbeing, allowing you to make a conscious decision to no longer contribute to the collective pain.

Most of us will admit to knowing of a dark place within our minds that is best left well enough alone. This is the playground of counselors and therapists. But most of us are doing okay. We're managing to function, so why would we want to look under that rock? The Pain Body, or the emotional aspect of the ego, takes the form of an individualized energy in the psyche of the each person. Our Pain Body is residual negative energy of our previous lifetimes, contributed to in the present lifetime. Most of the time the Pain Body energy remains hidden in our unconscious mind, contributing to our basic responses and orientation to life. When triggered by the right circumstances, our Pain Body "wakes up." This means that our negative energy "personality self" takes over our thoughts. It is easy to identify this in someone you know well — those times when a person becomes irrational, a grimace falling over their face, changing their countenance and behavior to someone other than the person you think you know.

This may be harder to identify in yourself. The manifestations of the Pain Body become more subtle as you shine the light of consciousness into the depths of your mind. Uncovering and breaking free of our collective programming is like peeling off the layers of an onion. Deeply programmed thought patterns such as mistrust and paranoia are enmeshed in a web of intertwined and self-validating thinking. We have many ways of justifying why we feel and think the way we do.

In awakening your mind through these exercises, you become the Observer of your thoughts. As you go through your day, you watch and capture anything in your thoughts that reflects the unconsciousness programming of your individual or the collective Pain Body. For example, you may become aware of a thought that belies a feeling of impending doom, a negative expectation of performance from yourself or another, a bit of satisfaction upon hearing the story of someone's unhappy occurrence, et cetera. You begin to capture those thoughts and immediately transform them to heal that place in your mind.

As you become the Observer of your thoughts, you become less fearful of what you will find lurking in the depths of your mind. You begin to smile when you see a thought reminiscent of the Pain Body — "oh, there it is again!" You accept the Pain Body as a manifestation of our collective history, now become like a friend on your path to freedom and true creativity.[1]

---

[1] Tolle, Eckhart. *A New Earth.*

Obsession — Compulsive Thinking

These repetitive and circular thoughts do not serve my
Highest Good. These thoughts are not Who I Am.

* * * * * * *

I am learning to live in the Now. I am capable of solving any
problem or resolving any situation.

* * * * * * *

I open my mind to a Higher Source of Direction.
I allow the undoing of events and experiences
that trigger this pain in my mind.

* * * * * * *

Every painful thought is replaced by a new and better
thought in my mind. I accept that I am healed.

~~~~~~

*Obsessive or repetitive thinking may result when your mind seeks an
outlet for excessive mental energy. Those who suffer this anguish may
find release in physical activity, or may seek chemical release through
alcohol or drugs. Obsessive thoughts often focus on your unworthiness or
inadequacy. These thoughts may take the form of generalized anxiety or
fear, worry about a seemingly irresolvable problem or situation, a repetition
of anger toward another person or toward yourself, or myriad other forms.
Such unproductive thinking is a trick of the ego-self that derails you from
taking positive action in the Now. Repetition of the statements included
in this affirmation support a process through which you begin to separate
yourself from identification with these thoughts.*

Bitterness — Hard-Heartedness

There is no person, situation, or set of conditions
that causes me to shut down or close myself off.

* * * * * * *

No matter what I witness, I am safe in the *Love of God* that
encompasses all things.

* * * * * * *

The same Light of Love that bathes my heart extends to
all persons experiencing hopelessness, fear,
pain, or struggle.

* * * * * * *

I offer all disturbing images to *Divine Grace* for healing.

We feel vulnerable when we witness something shocking or horrible. Memory of our own bad experiences also makes us lose Trust. Fear-based thinking may drive us to narrow our focus of concern to our own community or group, our family, or only ourselves — any domain where we imagine we have a chance to exercise control. Somewhere along the way, we realize it is stressful and exhausting to resist what we see or to attempt to enclose ourselves in a fortress of denial. Nor do we have to be the personal savior in every situation. It takes only a fraction of a moment to open-heartedly observe and silently offer everything disturbing we see to Divine Spirit for blessing.

Jealousy — Envy

The fate of all others is my fate. The Joy of all others is my
Joy. The Abundance and Joy of [person] is an extension of
my Abundance and Joy.

* * * * * * *

The Abundance and Joy of [person] is a testimonial of the
Abundance and Joy that is also mine to receive.

* * * * * * *

Everything of Light, Love, Prosperity, Abundance, Peace
experienced by others is an *extension of God's Kingdom*[1] and
thus is also experienced by me.

* * * * * * *

My Good Fortune brings Delight to all in my path.
My Bounty and Joy are a testament of *God's Grace* which
extends without judgment to each and every person.

---

*Feeling of envy or resentment at another's good fortune arises from our
mental programming of the reality of lack and limitation. We believe we
must fight and compete to achieve our goals. We believe something that
comes to another takes away something from us. Explore the deep roots of
these ideas in your own mind!*

---

[1] Foundation for Inner Peace. *A Course in Miracles.*

Anxiety — Fear — Dread

This feeling of anxiety comes out of the meaningless world
and not from my own Mind.

* * * * * * *

Feelings of fear and dread are an invitation
to deeper Understanding.

* * * * * * *

When I experience these feelings, I discover and come to
rely on my deeper strengths.

* * * * * * *

I remember the Truth of Who I Really Am and my place in
the awakening world.

These feelings are pervasive and subtle, operating on a subconscious level as the defining energies of our world. The degree to which you have mastered or become free of the struggle with fear identifies the degree to which your life experience is that of an actualized person versus one who is victimized in the world. Through practice of Presence, or being in the Now, your pain body dissipates.[1] Through gentleness and encouragement, you begin to separate yourself and move into a new way of being in the world.

---

[1] Tolle, Eckhart.. *A New Earth.*

Anger

No person or situation causes my anger. My own
suppressed needs cause the anger to arise within me.

* * * * * * *

I compassionately communicate my feelings and needs.

* * * * * * *

I offer all anger to *Divine Source* for healing. The heat of
anger within me evaporates like a puff of mist
into the atmosphere.

* * * * * * *

The message of anger is removed from the energy centers
and cells of my body.

* * * * * * *

Anger is an insignificant pulse of energy that flits briefly
across my mind, no longer triggering a response in me.

*Anger is a trigger that awakens your Pain Body to usurp control of your
thoughts and actions.[1] A first step toward freedom is to refrain from
projecting blame or cause onto another person or situation, instead exploring
inside yourself for a need that is not being met.[2] These statements are
targeted to changing your thoughts and behavior in response to anger, as
well as to removing the residue of anger stored in your energy body and
physical body.*

---

[1] Tolle, Eckhart. *A New Earth.*
[2] Rosenberg, Marshall. *Nonviolent Communication.*

Imagining Problems — Paranoia

Something is a problem only as I define it so. I do not require problems to solve in order to have self-worth.

* * * * * * *

I am Master of my experience. I am not subject to random forces in the Universe. Everything that happens in my world contributes to my wellbeing.

* * * * * * *

All beliefs that my Brother could wish to do me harm are healed in *Divine Light*.

* * * * * * *

My mind chooses new ideas about my Brother and Myself that allow me to share my Light with the World.

* * * * * * *

I draw to myself experiences and people that sustain me, support me, and affirm the gifts I bring to others and others bring to me.

Our egoic mind enjoys having problems because it makes us feel important. Solving problems makes us feel proud. Attracting or creating problems holds you in old patterns of response and deters you from your progress. Paranoia is another expression of fear rooted in the belief that the universe is a hostile place. This belief can be changed by opening your heart to Love, and accepting Grace.

Isolation — Feeling Disconnected

I courageously explore this feeling of isolation
to uncover the meaning it has for me.

* * * * * *

I discover the all-embracing *Divine Love* that emanates
from within my Soul.

* * * * * *

I connect with the *Universal Intelligence* within me.
I know that I am never alone.

* * * * * *

My Soul is connected to the Souls of all others as we
journey together toward Truth.

* * * * * *

My Universe is a friendly place. I greet every stranger as a
friend and I receive *Love* beyond measure.

Not wanting to connect with others, isolating oneself, indicates a pattern of deep suffering. A soul in this degree of pain is ready to experience a breakthrough. A sense of deep aloneness, even in the midst of a crowd, is intrinsic to the human condition. The sufferer may also view himself as living in a hostile universe — with the inevitable consequences that viewpoint attracts. It is impossible for us to choose loneliness and isolation once we have opened ourselves to experience the Divine Energy that lives inside each of us.

Infinite Sadness

I accept and carry this feeling of sorrow as I go about
my day, not needing to understand or fix it.

* * * * * * *

I carry this mournful feeling as if a fragile babe,
so precious, so vulnerable. I cry as the world cries.

* * * * * * *

I offer this feeling to *Divine Love*, allowing for the Time
when all tears shall cease.

* * * * * * *

Recognizing the Universal Pain of Existence, I bless
the world and everyone I meet today.

I remember, in my early twenties, reveling with college buddies in the intense anguish that seemed to dwell in our souls, as if we wore some badge of honor for the trials we had been through. The origin of this feeling was vague, given that we were from relatively privileged backgrounds and had experienced little true suffering at that point in our lives. We dubbed it "Infinite Sadness" — a connection to the pathos of life. A major purpose of our mind seems to be to distract us from exploring this. How could any ordinary human being bear to look at the depth of suffering here on Earth? In this set of affirmations, we bless this shrouded awareness, reminding ourselves that this is the world we made. You accept an invitation to elevate yourself, knowing that all suffering is transcended when the Christ Consciousness is awakened within you.

Indecision — Immobility — Depression

I give this decision over to God to instruct me as to the correct action or response.

* * * * * * *

I know what to do when the time is right.

* * * * * * *

I now break through that which blocks my clarity about my next step.

* * * * * * *

I recover my direction by seeking my Joy in the Present Moment.

* * * * * * *

I rediscover my Enthusiasm and Direction.

Chronic indecision or immobility in the face of problems is an invitation to sit quietly and unify your thoughts as to what it is you really want. Indecision also results when multiple "personality selves" flood your mind with so many competing possibilities that you cannot discern from amongst them what you wish to choose as the next activity or action. A need for perfection also stymies action.

Depression is a deep soul sickness that is pervasive in our society. Chemical therapies may be effective in creating a short-term break from the symptoms so that spiritual healing (self-healing) can take place. Depression may also result when we have forgotten that action only needs to take place in the present moment, and the right action is always that which increases Joy and Peace.

Resentment — Betrayal

I forgive and let go of all resentment. I incorporate the
learning in this situation to improve my life.

* * * * * * *

I accept that [this person] behaved in the best way
that they could in the situation,
according to their Understanding.

* * * * * * *

I let go of all ideas that I could be betrayed without my
agreement on some level to play that role.

* * * * * * *

I set myself free of old agreements. All karmic conditions
are fulfilled between this person and myself.

* * * * * * *

I experience myself as a new person in this moment.

*In the case of betrayal or other situations resulting in deep anger or
resentment toward another person, we are reaping the result of things
set in motion by our past actions or beliefs. Instead of pursuing years of
psychoanalysis, you can set yourself free by resolving to explore inwardly for
any lesson, proclaiming your intention to be reborn in the Present Moment.*

Restlessness — Dissatisfaction

I come into the Present Moment, and receive from this
dissatisfaction the message that is there for me.

* * * * * * *

I thank my mind for its effectiveness in solving problems.
I NOW take a break from problem-solving.

* * * * * * *

I am overwhelmed with Appreciation for the Abundance
that is mine in this lifetime.

*The egoic self rules through continually finding something that is wrong
with the present situation, something that needs fixing. Our mind then
keeps a running chain of thought focused on "how to solve this problem."
You may feel very purposeful and self-satisfied when your mind is thus
engaged. But on a deeper level, you know that somewhere real life is
happening and you are missing out. You capture a moment of bliss in sex,
a wonderful laugh at a party, a heartfelt cry watching a television show.
Is that all there is?*

*When the ego is in charge, a feeling of restlessness or dissatisfaction serves
to distract us from experiencing the bliss of living in the Present Moment.
We maintain a focus on Doing rather than Being. But no matter how
effective your mental chatter is in assuring that you do not fall in Love
with Life again, the "still small voice" inside never gives up attempting
to capture your attention long enough to give you precious glimpses of
your True Self. That is the message of Love that feeds your soul's longing!*

Addiction — Craving

I am Whole, Complete, and Perfect and do not require anything to bring me closer to Wholeness (Holiness).

* * * * * *

I let go of the illusionary search for a better feeling.

* * * * * *

I am open to receiving the lesson in my desire for [substance/situation/feeling].

* * * * * *

I release my desire for [substance/situation/feeling] to the Universe for Healing, knowing it IS removed from me in a way that serves my Highest Good.

In traditional cultures, certain drugs and alcohol are used as sacred vehicles to awaken the mind. Many who use alcohol or drugs are spiritual seekers. Certain drugs or experiences temporarily release your consciousness from the prison of the fear-based world. You gain an experiential memory of a freedom you would like to have more of in your life. The problem comes when you identify the substance or experience — even a guru — as the vehicle to the new feeling. As soon as you are dependent on that person or substance to give you that better feeling, you have replaced your former mental prison with a new one. In becoming free, you realize that you are already where you want to be, and you no longer need any vehicle to get you there.[1]

---

[1] Dyer, Wayne. *Being in Balance* (CD)

CHAPTER FOUR

EMPOWERING HEALTH
AND VITALITY

In order to heal one has to relax. This is the most important requirement for healing. When you are tense and tight, cellular vibration will be abnormal, and this will affect the functions, coordination, and balance of the organs and systems. This imbalance sustains illness and impedes healing.... Only when you are relaxed can your cells vibrate actively and in balance. When this happens, healing is supported and promoted.

Zhi Gang Sha, *Power Healing*

Interlude

Learning to Talk to Your Body

Affirmations in the first three chapters improve the character of your thoughts, developing positive states of mind. You deny and reverse destructive thoughts such as anger, resentment, bitterness, and all related negative emotions and feelings, because these energy patterns cause discord in the physical organism (as well as in your life experience). In this chapter, you utilize affirmations to support the perfect functioning of your physical body.

Positive states of mind raise your vibrational frequency, connecting you with your *Divine Nature*, which is *Love*. Your *Divine Self* knows only health. Love and the greater work of Love is the most potent healing power. Love is the most powerful physician of the universe.

The body is a tool, the sacred temple that houses your Spirit. When you realize that *Divine Energy* flows in and through all things, you reawaken your communication with the *Soul Presence* that exists within all of the components and subcomponents of your body. This *Soul Presence* is responsive to your thoughts. You become increasingly aware of your mind/body connection. The cellular reconstruction and functioning of the body take on the imprint of the mind.

At the same time, you know that every cell of your body, every organ, and every system of your body is an organism finely attuned within itself. You breathe and your hearts beat, your body systems function, without your directing them to do so. We know medically that the body is self-renewing. Regardless of what may have manifested through errors of your thinking (in this lifetime or in previous lifetimes), every cell and component of your body contains information for its perfect functioning. Your affirmations stimulate restoration to this state of perfection.

All healing is self healing. In empowering yourself for healing, do not eschew the medical professionals and the wonderful advancements of medical technology. When you visit the doctor, or receive an intervention in the hospital, take your consciousness of your oneness with *God* into that experience. You affirm that only Love flows through the doctors and those working with you for your healing. You ask questions to acquire as much information as possible about the physiology and pathology of your affliction. The more you learn, the better you can visualize and affirm your healing.

Through your affirmations, you begin to take charge of your thoughts and the direction of your mind. To maintain your health and vitality, you mentally travel through your body, sending love to the parts needing upliftment. When you are faced with illness, you say "hello" to the afflicted part of the body, affirming its perfection and directing your absolute and total love into the area. You call forth and affirm *Soul Presence* throughout all the components and subcomponents of your body. You deny weakness, illness, lack, or limitation.

Love active in consciousness overcomes error states of mind, restoring health and vitality, taking form in the body through each individual's consciousness.

Total Body Awakening

Every DNA/RNA strand

every cell, every organ,

every tissue, every nerve,

every fluid, every bone,

every muscle, every fiber,

every system, every membrane

every humor of my body

is responding to and is the result of

perfect instructions

reflecting the highest manifestation of the

creative energy of God in action —

in evidence — as ME

~~~~~~

While repeating this affirmation, visualize the components of your body temple lighting up as you mention them. Write this affirmation down and place it on an altar or in your prayer box, where it will continue to send a powerful "hello" to your body, rejuvenating from the inside out.

Rejuvenation at the Cellular Level (commentary)

Energy Medicine has given rise to a new theory of health and illness. Cells, organs, and body systems vibrate constantly, creating energy fields around themselves. These energy fields occupy the body spaces outside the cells, organs, and systems. The entire body also has an energy field, known as the aura. Illness results when there is an imbalance of energy flow at the cellular level, organ level, or body system level. On the level of the cell, there is continual transformation of matter and energy taking place. When cells expand, energy in the space is converted into matter inside the cell. When cells contract, matter inside the cell is transformed into energy in the space. When this transformation takes place in relative balance, there is health. In this way, energy and matter respond to "message," or direction through thought. Negative or destructive thought produces energy blockage and damage to cells. Eighty-five to ninety percent of illnesses are caused by too much energy in the space between the cells. Ten to fifteen percent of illnesses are the result of too little energy in the space.[1] Harmonious thought restores balance to the flow between matter and energy, promoting regeneration and healing.

---

[1] Sha, Zhi Gang. *Soul, Mind, Body Medicine.*

Rejuvenation at the Cellular Level

I send love and blessing to all the cells of my body.

* * * * * * *

All cells of my body reproduce in accordance with *Divine*
instructions for total health and wholeness.

* * * * * * *

All cells of my body receive and process the nutrients
needed to do the work they are programmed to do.

* * * * * * *

Expansion and contraction of my cells, the transformation
between matter and energy, occurs in perfect balance
in every cell and organ of my body.

* * * * * * *

Cells that are overstimulated return to perfect vibration;
stuck energy between cells is released.
Abnormal cells are destroyed by my immune system
and are replaced by normal cells.

* * * * * * *

My cells function in perfect balance until such time as the
animating energy chooses to leave this body.

Inner Beauty

Deep inside my physical body, I experience my
Divine Body, sitting in serene contemplation.

* * * * * *

I Am the Jewel in the Lotus.

* * * * * *

I radiate the beauty of my Infinite Self, and it is this that
others see when they look at me.

* * * * * *

I am a mirror of the inner beauty in everything and
everyone I encounter.

*As you focus your attention inward, you become aware of your "inner
body" or your "aliveness."[1] You begin to align with your true self as the
"small person" inside your abdomen (or wherever your soul has established
its home in your body).[2] There you expand to envision yourself as a being
of light, exquisitely beautiful, fluid and flowing. What a joy it is to move
beyond limiting concepts of physical attractiveness and the need to validate
or condemn superficial aspects of ourselves or others.*

[1] Tolle, Eckhart. *A New Earth.*
[2] Sha, Zhi Gang. *Soul, Mind, Body Medicine.*

Youthfulness — Long Life

I let go of all ideas of Time and Aging that are prevalent in
this world.

* * * * * * *

I am willing to serve in this domain as long as it is
Right for me to do so.

* * * * * * *

I am ageless, timeless, serene, creating myself
in the Image of the *Eternal All That Is*.

* * * * * * *

The date of my physical birth carries no meaning,
as I now agree to continue in this body
outside of the definition of Time.

* * * * * * *

I now join the Old Ones, responding to instructions
emanating from another Reality. And So It Is.

---

*The idea that no one lives on earth more than one hundred (or so) years is
a collective belief we hold; thus it is a choice we make. It is possible to free
yourself from ideas about aging in the same way you free yourself from
other beliefs held in the subconscious that limit who you think you are.*[1]

[1] Chopra, Deepak. *Ageless Body, Timeless Mind*.

Calling Forth Energy

I know that all Energy is derived from *Source* and
Source is Infinite.

* * * * * * *

I command NOW the flow of Lifeforce to vibrate
throughout my body,
encompassing every cell from my feet to the crown of my
head in perfect balance of matter and energy
within and without,
cleansing and renewing my body's Energy Field.

* * * * * * *

I am prepared for the tasks of this day.

These statements activate prana or chi (universal life force energy) for those occasions when it is important to function at your best for a particular event or task at hand. Perfect balance of Energy and Matter inside and outside the cells is established, as well as balance of the energy field, or aura, surrounding the body. These affirmations are particularly powerful in combination with a movement activity such as yoga, tai chi, or stretching. Energy will be activated in your body and you will have stamina to accomplish your goals without relying on stimulants such as caffeine. At the conclusion of the event or activity, it is advisable to give thanks for the energy boost and invite relaxation and rest.

Relaxation — Rest

I embrace this time of rest; I am free of thought.

* * * * * * *

As I relax in the Now, my body's systems, cells,
and organs are bathed in healing light.

* * * * * * *

There is nothing I must do.

* * * * * * *

I now restore my energy for the delightful activities
that await me.

When you are in tune with your inner Being, your energy cycles naturally between periods of activity and periods of rest. It is important to allow your energy to rise and fall in accordance with internal and external rhythms, to maintain the body's balance and protect yourself from overactivity, overexcitement, or burnout. You may struggle with thoughts that you haven't done enough, the need to accomplish more, fear of falling behind, ideas that you do not deserve to rest. Insomnia is the unfortunate result when we deny the blessed gift of rest.

Perfect Functioning of Immune System

I give thanks to all components of my Immune System for
perfect protection of my body's cells, organs,
and structures.

* * * * * * *

A perfect boundary to my inner body is maintained by
my skin and the fluids protecting all openings. Inside my
body, healthy cells and infected cells are correctly labeled,
recognized, and responded to.

* * * * * * *

My Thymus, Spleen, Lymph System, Bone Marrow,
and all components of my Immune System
function according to perfect instructions.

* * * * * * *

All white blood cells in my body
respond to Message, produce antibodies, and interact with
one another to maintain my perfect health.

───────────────────────

*Most of us entered life with an immune system that functions according
to perfect instructions (Message) encoded in our energy field,, were it not
for the interference of our thoughts. The work undertaken by the many
components of your immune system to maintain balance and health inside
your body every day is extraordinary! A corollary to this is to instruct
the mind to reduce stress-producing thoughts, which place the body in a
state of readiness for action ("fight or flight") and deter energy away from
essential operations of the immune system.*

Perfect Metabolism — Relationship with Food

My mind receives perfect information about nutrients it needs to sustain my unique constitution.

* * * * * * *

My intake of food and drink provides energy that sustains the activities of my body and mind.

* * * * * * *

All organs and secretions of my digestive system function according to perfect instructions.

* * * * * * *

Blood circulation, delivery of food, fluid, and oxygen to cells and organs, transformation of nutrient into matter in the cells, balance of matter in the cells and energy in the space between cells, all function in perfect order.

* * * * * * *

I am aware and choose what and when I eat or drink, whether for sustenance or for pleasure of sensation.

By exploring and owning your unique constitution, you discover the combination of foods and exercise that best generates your healthiest bodily expression in the world.

Clarity and Balance

I am grounded through all my chakras
as I walk with ease and confidence in the world.

* * * * * *

I welcome the experience of clear sight that comes
when I focus my awareness in the center of my head.

* * * * * *

Energy flows and circulates throughout the meridians
of my body to create perfect balance.

* * * * * *

The mechanisms of my inner ear function flawlessly,
transmitting correct messages to my brain
and sensory organs.

* * * * * *

My mind expands with clarity and lightness,
radiating balance and harmony throughout my Being.

Vertigo or lightheadedness can occur when a person's energy is "ungrounded" or concentrated in the upper chakras (energy centers of the body). Migraine headaches, along with vertigo or labyrinthitis, often manifest when the intuitive center (Third Eye) is developing or opening in people who are in a state of inner conflict or resistance to the flowering of that gift. The use of affirmations encourages the blossoming of intuition, with concomitant subsiding of debilitating episodes.

Strengthening the Heart

I love my heart, the message center of my body.
Thank you, my heart, for perfect functioning.

* * * * * *

My heart is the powerhouse of my body, the supreme
energy station, the provider, the sustainer of life.

* * * * * *

My heart is the seat and center of the experience,
understanding, and expression of the LOVE of *God*
that I reflect back into the world.

* * * * * *

My heart — its muscle; its vessels; the electrical signals it
receives and transmits; its communication with my lungs,
my blood, and all the cells, tissues, and organs of my body —
ALL are responding to perfect instructions
of the perfect Energy of God creating with me
and through me.

*Meditation within the Heart chakra facilitates the awakening of
Unconditional (Universal) Love. This affirmation for the heart also lends
support in the situation of depression or its corollary, overexcitement.*[1]

[1] Sha, Zhi Gang. *Soul, Mind, Body Medicine.*

Strengthening the Lungs

I love my lungs. I say hello to my Lungs, where I receive
and exchange the Breath of Life.

* * * * * *

I awaken to awareness of the rising and falling,
the continual motion that defines and creates all Life.

* * * * * *

My lungs contribute to perfect balance of water
in my body. Thank you, my lungs.

* * * * * *

My nasal passages, trachea, lungs, alveoli and all pathways
of respiration are repaired of damage,
cleared of blockages, and function according to
perfect instructions.

* * * * * *

I offer my grief to the *One Love* for healing. I breathe easily
and freely as I release the weight of sorrow.

---

*Breathing, along with all the other workings of our body, is directed by
the subconscious mind. Focusing on your breathing when you meditate
is a way of getting in touch with your "inner body" and experiencing
Presence.*[1] *Breath is the animating Divine Principle. Our soul soars away
on the breath when we leave this body. The lungs are also known to be the
locus of grief and sadness.*[2]

---

[1] Tolle, Eckhart. *A New Earth.*
[2] Sha, Zhi Gang. *Soul, Mind, Body Medicine.*

Cleansing of Impurities

I say hello to the system that cleanses my bodies organs,
cells, and tissues.

* * * * * *

All waste products flow easily from my cells, tissues,
and organs into the surrounding space.

* * * * * *

All that does not belong or is not needed by my body's
cells, tissues, and organs is collected by the system of
cleansing and purification (small intestine, liver, kidneys,
blood, skin).

* * * * * *

All waste products of respiration, digestion, and metabolism
are evacuated from my body
through perfect functioning.

When your thoughts reside in the anxiousness of past or future, energy in your body is diverted to bones and muscles, in readiness for action. Here you turn inward to send love and validation to stimulate perfect functioning of all the cells and organs in your body related to cleansing and purification. In this way, the flow of energy is stimulated and balanced in the cells and organs, at the same time purging the body of toxins and other waste products.

Releasing Chronic Pain

My purpose for having this pain has been fulfilled.
I am ready to release it.

* * * * * * *

This pain is not a part of Who I Really Am. I separate
from this pain now.

* * * * * * *

A ball of bright golden light enters the area of my pain,
encircling and absorbing it.

* * * * * * *

The ball of bright golden light carries the pain outside of
my body where it is sails into the center of the Earth.

* * * * * * *

All trace of the memory of pain, all belief that this pain is
necessary or deserved, is NOW erased from my mind.

Chronic pain is the result of an energy imbalance or stuck energy. The pain may become so familiar that you expect it — you begin to define yourself by it. Sometimes you invite your pain to return when you notice that it is absent. Erasing the memory of the pain from the mind is essential.

Flexibility — Agility

My body moves with ease.

* * * * * * *

Through stretching, bending, walking, reaching, I increase
the flow of energy to all parts of my body.

* * * * * * *

All the joints of my body are fluid; the bones of my neck
and spine are in perfect alignment.

* * * * * * *

With gratitude and joy, I inhabit my flowing body.

While traversing the mid-life conditions of menopause and divorce, I sought to change my deeply-ingrained belief in the inevitability of aging, pain, and death. The answer came to me with profound clarity: Movement is life. Stop moving and decay begins. I became bored quickly with most exercise routines, but I loved music and loved to dance. Dancing is not appreciated or fostered in our culture. As with other forms of artistic expression, only those who approach some standard of perfection are lauded or even allowed to participate in these joys. Not having been born with the ideal of the perfect female body, I had closed down the subtle realms of motion that lived in my soul. I got rid of a lot of furniture, installed a laminate floor and wall mirrors in my living room, collected music that I loved, and began to dance for God. Those who knew me said I had been reborn. They were so right!

77

Weight Loss (commentary)

*First, you must determine the reason your weight is a problem for you —
something other than our cultural conditioning to be fashion-model thin. A
health issue may have arisen; you may not feel good carrying around those
extra pounds, or you may not want to have to buy new clothes! Then, you
make a decision to consciously create a new behavior pattern, in essence
becoming a new person. Your behavior may not change immediately as
you lapse into taking unconscious actions. As you learn to stay present
and observe your behavior, you uncover the root thoughts that spur you
to consume unconsciously.*

Weight Loss

My thoughts direct me to the perfect intake of nutrients
needed for the cells of my body to perform their work.

* * * * * *

I am no longer compelled to consume something in order
to feel happy or to stimulate my mind.

* * * * * *

Excess matter causing distress in my body is now
converted into a form that is shed and released.

* * * * * *

Fat cells in my body are transformed
and return to normal cells.
Perfect balance of eating, digestion, and
metabolism is restored.

* * * * * *

I experience lightness in my body as my cellular vibration
increases and I attain my perfect weight.

Enjoying Your Sexuality (commentary)

~~~~~~

Our bodies are exquisite vessels for experiencing and sharing sensual and sexual delight. For many of us, sexual exchange, with its momentary ecstasy, has been the only vehicle that brings us to be fully in the NOW. It is no wonder that sex has been viewed as the supreme act, or goal, of life on this planet. All communication through bodies is holy and sacred, bringing you into union with another person and with God. Yet in this world of duality, sex can also be used as a vehicle for the horrific. As with any form of meditation, it is important to set the intention and create protected space for this activity. The body is a vehicle for experiencing release from duality, evaporation of personhood, as well as sublime union with the eternal Now. Once you know this, you can honor sexual delight as a signpost directing you to expanding realms of wonder and contentment.

Enjoying Your Sexuality

My body is a sacred vehicle for experiencing Presence.

* * * * * * *

Through my body I participate in the Divine
Creative Process.

* * * * * * *

I am encircled with Loving Protection. Nothing that intends
pain or harm can invade my body or enter
my thoughts.

* * * * * * *

I join with my Beloved in the place of No Mind,
united with *All That Is.*

* * * * * * *

My spirit is rejuvenated through pleasurable sensations of
touch and energy exchange.

* * * * * * *

Through the vehicle of my body, my spirit gives birth to
energy that transforms this world.

Heightening Your Sense Perception (commentary)

To the mystic, the senses are tools with which the Divine expresses through us. The body's purpose is to serve as a vehicle of communication to restore our connection with our Source. All interactions through the senses have the potential to move us forward in our journey home. When our eyesight fails, we are entertaining ideas that we have seen all there is to see, that no new glory awaits us through the wonder of our eyes beholding. Loss of hearing is a reflection of thoughts that there is nothing we do not already know, that there is no new information or idea we wish to receive through the spoken word. We can boldly apply affirmations to repair and augment the sensory apparatus of our bodies.

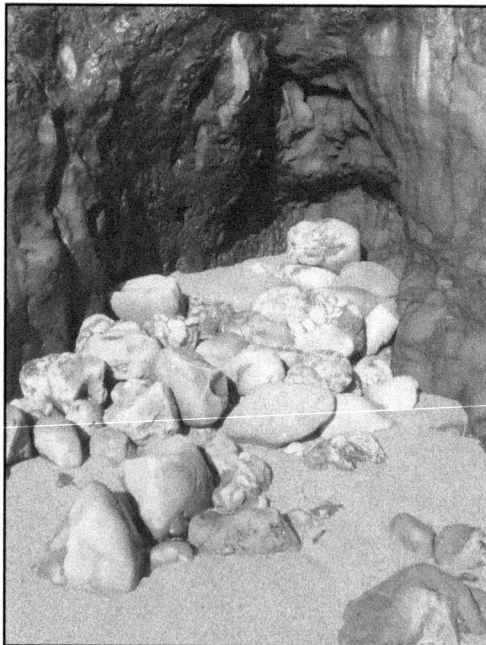

Improving Vision

My eyes, and all structures and signals that contribute to my
vision, function according to perfect instructions.

* * * * * *

My cornea remains flexible and focuses easily
between viewing near and far.

* * * * * *

All impairments to my vision are repaired. I see clear,
crisp, vividly colorful images.

* * * * * *

I take delight in the panorama of physical form.

Improving Hearing

My ears, and all structures and signals that contribute to my hearing, function according to perfect instructions.

* * * * * *

All impairments to my hearing are repaired. I receive clear messages across a broad range of frequencies.

* * * * * *

I give reverence to Sound as the original vehicle calling Form out of the Formless.

* * * * * *

I embrace the exquisite realm of sound in music, voice, nature, and the hum that is the vibration of the Universe.

Preparing for a Doctor's Visit

I am prepared to receive information or treatment
that will help me toward my goal of perfect health.

* * * * * * *

Traffic is easy and I arrive in plenty of time.

* * * * * * *

I find parking easily. I feel confident and centered.
I am called within moments of taking my seat.

* * * * * * *

The staff and nurses are relaxed and friendly.
My doctor is grounded and attentive to my needs.

* * * * * * *

I remain focused in my listening.
I understand and remember the instructions I receive.

* * * * * * *

The medical professionals are partners in my self-healing.
Restoration of my perfect health is assured.

It is easy to be distracted during a visit to the doctor or the hospital. If you are receiving important instruction, it is best to take a family member or friend with you. Bring a small tape recorder or Dictaphone if you have one, and ask the doctor for her permission to record her instructions. Affirmations are a powerful tool to prepare you for treatment or surgery, as well as to accelerate the process of recovery.

Healing After Surgery

God's healing light fills every cell of my body.

* * * * * *

Every organ remembers and responds
to its perfect instructions.

* * * * * *

All processes by which the body nurtures itself
and eliminates what it does not need
return to perfect functioning.

* * * * * *

I embrace my energy and enthusiasm.

* * * * * *

I am open to a new definition of my life
and my purpose.

* * * * * *

I am joy-filled and grateful to be born again.

Affirmations are powerful tools to assist in preparing your mind and body to receive surgery, and for recovery following surgery. Recorded affirmations of relaxation and healing can be played on headphones during surgery. The above statements were written for recovery following surgery to remove the gallbladder. Modify the statements to invoke the healing conditions appropriate to the intervention.

CHAPTER FIVE

FLOWING AT HOME

You are using a principle of thought which is similar to this principle in Physics: Action and reaction are equal to the thoughts themselves. When you BECOME ONE with ideas which are for your positive welfare, not against it, you may be certain that is what you will experience. When you become the consciousness of what you want, it appears, as event. Your event!!

Jay Scott Neale, *What the Great Have Thought, You Can Think!*

Interlude

Learning to Work with Infinite Power

Whether you live with a partner, share your life with family, or live alone, your home is your private sanctuary, a place that nurtures your soul. Home is a place to practice letting go of beliefs in limitation and lack as you open to abundance and prosperity. Once you know you can easily address basic requirements for comfort, and do what you need to do to comply with the rules of society without effort and striving, your spirit is energized for the experience of companionship, the expression of creativity, and the joy of pure being.

When you view the tasks of daily life as a problem or a challenge, you become subject to deeply programmed rules and limiting beliefs about yourself and the physical world. Fundamental to your remembering how to live with grace and ease is to awaken your connection with the quantum realm — that place where energy interacts in nonlinear fashion and instantaneous results are possible. The affirmations in this chapter are a practical way to connect and experience *Infinite Power* as you manifest your desires for abundance and prosperity, safety for those you love, physical comfort, right livelihood, and nurturing relationships.

A technique known as "Prayer Treatment" is taught to all practitioners of mental science. Those starting out are encouraged to use Prayer Treatment to manifest more tangible, mundane things. The results or "demonstrations" that occur in the ordinary physical world begin to satisfy the need of your logical mind for substantive *proof*. As your practice matures, you come to know and manifest the greater gifts that bring you delight far beyond a new car or the right house. The basic Prayer Treatment consists of five steps:

Basic Prayer Treatment

Step One — Affirm that God is in Everything

Sit quietly. Get into a peaceful state of mind, happy to be here. If it works for you, visualize a place that brings you peace and joy. Affirm that God Is Present In All Things in the Universe. Express your deep conviction that God is the only Power there is, the Power that heals through Love, making all things new and perfect.

Step Two — Affirm that You are in God and God is in You

Now that you have affirmed that God is in all things in the Universe, make a place for yourself in that Universe and feel the *Presence of God* coursing throughout your body, in every thought, and in every domain of your life.

Step Three — Make Your Request for Guidance, Aid, Healing

Here you affirm what it is you want this *Power* to do in your life. State your requests in the present tense, as if you have already received what it is you are asking for. Focus on how you *feel* to have achieved what you desire, rather than on details of how it will happen.

Step Four — Express Praise and Gratitude to the Divine Workforce

Give thanks to the *Infinite Power* for responding to your requests. Raise your vibration with rejoicing! Your expression of gratitude sets the energy in motion to accomplish the goals. Know that *Divine Action* is underway to meet your requests.

Step Five — Release

Let go of all doubt. If you visualize, put the energy of your request into a glowing ball of light and see it float away from you into the Universe. "In perfect confidence, I let go and allow the *Infinite Power* to work in my life." Amen. And So It Is.

****

Other possible inclusions in this process:

Denial — If you sense resistance to what you are requesting, it is useful to include a Denial between Steps Three and Four. A Denial is an emphatic statement that there is nothing in the Universe or in life that can have power over or oppose this request.

Forgiveness — A statement of forgiveness is very powerful inserted between Steps Two and Three. "I forgive myself for all my mistakes and forgive all others for actions or decisions I judged to be weakness or trespassing against me."

Prayer for Others — Prayers for others may be included following Step Three.

****

We remind ourselves that home is our kingdom, our personal playground. It is the place where, in contrast to work where we most likely are not the "big boss," we *are* in charge of our lives. The destiny of some of us is to achieve out in the world; for others it is to find fulfillment through service to the community; and for others, our home will be the setting for the journey to enlightenment. Our purpose is to evolve the essence of God, and that takes place independently of our environment, through an inner journey.

Affirmations such as those in this chapter set us on the path to empowering ourselves in our daily life, opening us to trust as we awaken the knowledge of our Divine heritage.

Blessing for Home

Our home is a place of peace and harmony.

* * * * * * *

Communication is encouraged and we feel safe to share
our feelings.

* * * * * * *

We work together to manage the responsibilities
of daily life with grace and ease.

* * * * * * *

Each member of our household is encouraged and
honored for his or her unique talents and views.

* * * * * * *

What we need comes to us without strife and
each member of our household thrives and prospers.

---

*These simple statements create the energetic character of a home where
healthy communication takes place and the basic human needs of each
individual are met. Basic human needs are universal and include: Love,
Sustenance, Safety, Empathy, Honesty and Clarity, Autonomy, Celebration
and Play, Rest, Intimacy, Creativity, Community, Meaning and Purpose.
[1] You may feel compelled to add to this list of human needs following a
search within your heart. For me, the list needs Communion with Nature
(including pets). Construct your own affirmations to enhance the treasured
dimensions of your life.*

---

[1] Rosenberg, Marshall. *Nonviolent Communication: A Language of Life.*

Beginning the Day

It is wonderful to be alive!

I am centered and ready for this day.

Everything today will happen easily.

I am in the flow and nothing can upset me.

* * * * * *

Customized add-ons:

[Everyone I meet today has a message for me.]

[I am comfortable at this afternoon's gathering.]

[I accomplish many things on my TO DO list today.]

[I am especially loving to my partner today.]

As part of setting the energy for your day, take time to reflect on, or write down, some of your intentions or goals for the day. (Remember: Resting and relaxing are intentions too for today's busy people!) Create customized statements in support of your goals.

Perfect Partnership

My partner and I share deep common interests.
We discover many activities to enjoy together.

* * * * * * *

We enjoy communicating and we solve problems easily.

* * * * * * *

We make decisions together about important things such as
financial matters and raising the children.

* * * * * * *

We share a deep intimacy.

* * * * * * *

We create a perfect balance of togetherness
and independence that fosters our growth
individually and as a couple.

The primary love relationship provides a sacred mirror of who you are on your path to greatness. Observe your relationship and you will see that it is constantly changing. There is nothing that does not deserve attention in a relationship if one of the partners thinks it does. Customize these statements to reflect what is most important in your relationship. Areas that are challenges are great targets for affirmations. These statements affirm what is true and bring more of it; alternatively, they send a message of what you wish for into the Field to attract matching energy. State your desire with focus, and watch a shift occur with seemingly no explanation. Grasp any opportunity that opens to strengthen your partnership!

Accomplishing Goals

I accomplish [my goal] with energy, enthusiasm,
and an attitude of playfulness.

* * * * * *

I receive direction from within when it is the right time to
move forward on [my goal] and what action to take.

* * * * * *

I am flexible and readjust my thinking
when things change or don't go according to my plan.

* * * * * *

Everything is accomplished in the right and perfect way.

Running your home life is the same as running a business. To be in the flow of abundance requires attention to understand what IS, affirm what you want, give it to God, and then know that it is done. Affirmations work well for manifesting changes you desire in the physical world. Be awake to see the cues and prepared to take action as the outcomes of your choices appear in your world.

Friendships Outside the Home

My life enriches the lives of others, who in turn
enrich my life.

* * * * * * *

My life is shared with companions who are drawn to me for
a reason, a season, or a lifetime.

* * * * * * *

I attract new people into my life in whose company
I feel comfortable, stimulated, and cherished.

*Sometimes too much absorption in our household matters causes us to lose
perspective and become moody or irritable. We require quality relationships
outside the home to maintain a balanced psyche. These statements address
the feeling of wanting more interaction with friends in your life. The
converse of this affirmation is feeling exhausted and overwhelmed by people
who are drawing from your energy, in which case there is a need to create
some space and time for yourself.*

Getting in the Flow of Your Abundance

I draw Abundance from the Universal Flow of Wealth
that is the gift of *Divine Intelligence* to all creation.

* * * * * * *

I lovingly attend to my finances, directing inflow
and outflow, free of fear, according to my highest vision.

* * * * * * *

The stream of wealth pouring into my life always exceeds
that which I need to manifest my grandest dreams.

* * * * * * *

In giving back to the *Source of My Supply*, I empower the
cycle of Abundance to flow in my world.

* * * * * * *

I joyfully pour out the gifts of my abundance to create
enjoyment of life for myself and those in my world.

---

*In Chapter Two (see page 31), we work through our deeply ingrained beliefs
in limitation and lack, along with feelings of guilt for our good fortune.
In the above statements, we focus on getting in the flow and embracing
the responsibility for managing our wealth in a compassionate way. The
concept of tithing is suggested here. The core principle that "you give to
receive" is present in the many books targeting prosperity consciousness
and wealth building.*

Making a Decision

I open a channel to my *Divine Source* of information.

* * * * * *

I experience clarity that allows me to explore my inner conflict about the course of action to take.

* * * * * *

I partner with my inner voice and open to Guidance in knowing what to do.

I reach a place of certainty about the deepest desire of my heart and the right action to take.

* * * * * *

I remain open and allow the unfolding of events to direct me in my decisions, knowing that all is well.

As you begin to examine the intention behind your choices, your actions become increasingly motivated by a desire for the highest good of all concerned. When we experience inner conflict about a decision, our ego in one of its many guises is at play in the situation. The process of living through affirmative thinking begins to restructure the deepest levels of our consciousness, making a fundamental shift in our approach to life. As we learn to partner with our Divine Intelligence, our disparate personality-selves become more integrated, and we move beyond the place of inner conflict. We know what is right to do. We joyfully arrive at the place of never having to make another decision.[1]

---

[1] Chopra, Deepak. *The Book of Secrets.*

Rebalancing — Summoning Energy

I clear myself of ideas that are not mine, needs that are
not mine, thoughts that do not serve me.

* * * * * *

All limiting conditions are released from my body
and my mind as I focus on the tasks at hand.

* * * * * *

I call forth personal Power from the wellspring deep within
my solar plexus to accomplish what I need to do.

* * * * * *

The energy field around my body is whole, cleansed, and
vibrating with light.

There are days when you know immediately upon waking that your energy seems to be off for some reason. The best thing you can do when this happens is to treat yourself gently throughout the day, attending to what you need to do, being careful not to place unnecessary demands on yourself. Limit your contact with others inside and outside the home so as not to create any additional disturbance to your psyche. Use these affirmations to cleanse your body and mind, and call upon the Universal Source of Energy to boost your strength in order to do the things you must do.

Encouraging Children to Thrive

I allow [child] to make decisions for herself
and invite her to communicate her needs and desires.

* * * * * * *

I let go of ideas that [child's] purpose is to meet my
expectations for appearance, personality, or performance.

* * * * * * *

I am open to exploring [child's] feelings about
the schedule of activities [amount of homework etc.]

* * * * * * *

I allow [child] to be different than me and encourage him to
express his gifts and talents in the world
in his own way.

Many children are being born on our Earth today who have special knowledge and gifts through which they will contribute to a shift in consciousness that is necessary for the survival of our planet. Whether or not we ourselves are parents or grandparents, children in some way impact all of our lives. Each one of us who expresses willingness will be given the opportunity to help nurture these young ones, as it is through the children that our world will be saved. In the affirmations on this and the following three pages, we shift our consciousness away from subjugation and force to an attitude of the highest respect and partnership with these special treasures in our lives.

Blessing for Children's Friendships

My child [name] draws friends who awaken

Joy and Laughter

Wisdom and Insight

Comfort and Kindness

in whose company many happy memories are created.

Children Thriving in School

My children [names] receive nurturing care
and attention at school.

* * * * * *

My children have experiences at school that help them
to know their worth and to appreciate others.

* * * * * *

My children receive learning experiences that help them
discover their unique gifts and talents.

* * * * * *

My children are blessed with friends and teachers who
help them explore and discover who they are
and the special way in which they contribute to life.

Every parent wants the best for their children, but our attention may fluctuate between not tuning in closely enough and becoming too interfering or heavy-handed. Instead of worrying or manipulating or forcing, you can employ affirmations to set up the energy for the success of your child. When you focus your mind toward a positive picture of the world your children inhabit day to day, the energy of your certainty and peace of mind unfolds in a concrete way in your children's experience.

Children's Confidence to Face Challenges

My child [name] draws to himself focus, confidence,
and energy to bring a perfect outcome.

* * * * * * *

My beloved child knows that she is never alone.

* * * * * * *

My beloved child knows that all the help he needs
is inside of himself.

* * * * * * *

My beloved child knows that no harm can come to her
because I am Here.

* * * * * * *

My beloved child understands that he will know
in the moment what is right to do or not to do.

* * * * * * *

My beloved child knows that she is enfolded
in loving arms until the end of time and that
I Am Always Here.

It is very disturbing to a parent when a child is worried or afraid. At the same time, such experiences are a vital part of the child's learning and need to be allowed to occur. These statements are powerful when spoken privately or with your child, set up an energy of self-assurance and comfort for both parents and children.

The sets of affirmations on the next five pages are examples of how affirmative statements can be created to express our intention and enhance the common experiences of daily life, such as entertaining, traveling, and gardening. Can affirmations be tailored to address a house remodeling project, finding a new car, adopting the perfect pet, coping with a visit from the in-laws, recovery from a fire or flood? What about getting rid of gophers? Of course! The only limit is your imagination.

Entertaining Guests at Home

All preparations come together easily
and in perfect timing.

* * * * * *

Our guests receive our home as a place of love and light.

* * * * * *

We share with our guests in meaningful ways that validate
who we are and enhance all of our lives.

* * * * * *

Time spent with our guests is enlivening and inspiring.

* * * * * *

Our guests find comfort and restoration of their spirits
in our company.

Having a Good Time at a Party

I am relaxed and centered in myself.
I mix easily with others and know just what to say.

* * * * * *

I am interested in listening to people's stories and
enjoy sharing something of who I am.

* * * * * *

I am confident in myself and experience no distress when
exposed to personalities very different than my own.

An Outing or Trip

Harmonious and joyful energy
surrounds the planning for this outing.

* * * * * *

The logistics of this outing fall into place
with a minimum of effort.

* * * * * *

Coordination of all the factors and people involved
happens naturally.

* * * * * *

Everyone's experience of the outing is enhanced through
enjoyment and sharing amongst all the participants.

Ease and Safety in Traffic

My Heavenly Protectors take charge of my vehicle
as I envision the path of my journey in a field of light.

* * * * * *

The way to my destination is clear of all obstacles.

* * * * * *

A zone of safety surrounds my vehicle.

* * * * * *

Each of the drivers sharing the road with me
finds a blessing in their day today.

Opening to New Adventures

I welcome new adventures. I am surrounded
with loving companionship and simpatico compatriots.

* * * * * *

I create home wherever I go. I am captivated
by new people and new experiences.

* * * * * *

I experience unsurpassed appreciation
of unexpected beauty.

* * * * * *

I am embraced in safety and protection.

* * * * * *

I experience supreme health and energy.
I find serene relaxation.

Easy Traveling

Details of our travel fall into place effortlessly. We are
prepared, relaxed, and centered as we leave our home.

* * * * * *

Any deviations from our plan happen for a reason
and we adjust easily.

* * * * * *

Our minds and bodies easily adjust to a shift in time zone
and the energy of a new and different place.

Bountiful Gardens

I welcome the Energy of growing, thriving…
the cycle of rebirth and change.

* * * * * * *

I am in awe to witness the release of oxygen… rock to soil
uniting with miraculous water and seed.

* * * * * * *

I welcome green, lush, pristine, marvelous beauty…
nourishing and nurturing our bodies and souls.

* * * * * * *

I revel in receiving from Earth this sustenance and majesty,
then returning to Earth what belongs to Earth.

For Fruiting Trees

Our beautiful fruit trees are blessed with perfect
nourishment and pollination.

* * * * * * *

We gratefully receive the bounty of perfect fruit,
free from blemishes.

* * * * * * *

The gift of this abundance is directed to loving use.

Coming to Terms with Deer and Gophers

We willingly accept our responsibility as caretakers
of this beautiful land.

* * * * * *

This land repels all that would feast upon its bounty
without invitation or attention to preserving
its productivity.

* * * * * *

The beautiful plants we cherish are invisible to all that
would harm them or destroy them.

* * * * * *

We invite these creatures to relocate in their right place,
where they are honored for their service rather than
despised for their destructiveness.

* * * * * *

We now announce the measures we will take to preserve
nature's beauty, knowing that such is a judgment.

* * * * * *

We hold that the Good outweighs the consequences.

There is no limit to appropriate subjects for our affirmations !

Creating Time or Space for Yourself

I create uninterrupted time and space to focus on my
projects, my dreams, my affirmations, and my visioning.

* * * * * * *

Finding time to nurture myself, I express gratitude
and let my Spirit freely resonate.

* * * * * * *

Others appreciate and support my need for alone time.

* * * * * * *

I surround myself with space and rest,
free from noise and stimulation.

* * * * * * *

I return into the company of others enriched, more able
to give love, more resilient, more able to receive love.

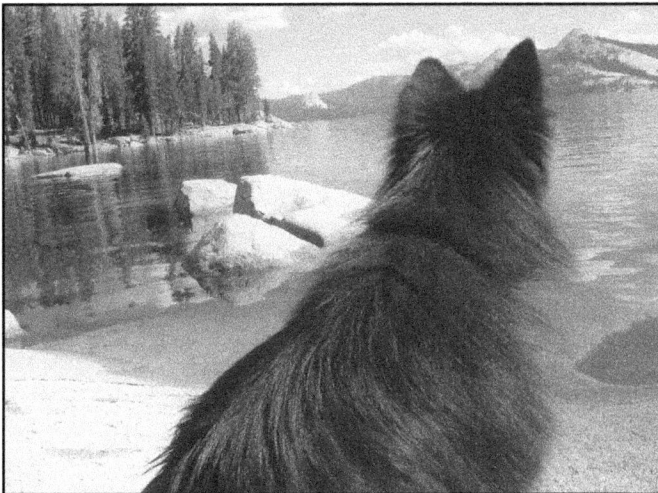

Ending the Day — Peaceful Sleep (commentary)

~~~~~~~~~~~~~~~~~~~~~~~~~~~~~~~~~~~~~~~

In sleep, we merge with Source and "draw from it the vital energy that sustains [us.]"[1] I am astonished at the number of my friends and family members who do not sleep well. Sleep disturbances are often attributed to hormonal changes, to stress or worry, or to aging. I prefer the thought that nighttime distress is a sign of our spiritual growth. As our awareness expands, we acquire more ability to connect with other dimensions of experience, such as the travels we take during sleep. It is natural for the egoic mind to resist sleep in the same way it battles with other aspects of our self-awakening. Sleep disturbance is evidence that you are changing, that you are emerging into a new way of being. You can bless this trouble, roll with it, fight the good fight, knowing that it is temporary.

---

[1] Tolle, Eckhart. *The Power of Now.*

Ending the Day — Peaceful Sleep

I give thanks for the events and experiences of this day.

* * * * * * *

I now draw my energy field in close around my body
and disconnect from the energy of others.

* * * * * * *

My mind is clear of all thoughts. Whatever is unresolved in
my mind I give to God.

* * * * * * *

The room where I sleep is grounded and protected
by the guardians of my spirit.

* * * * * * *

I experience deep relaxation as I touch my bed.
I fall into deep undisturbed sleep.

* * * * * * *

I awaken refreshed at the time I intend to wake
in the morning.

CHAPTER SIX

Healing our Relationships

If a woman is really upset, a man assumes she is blaming him. If she seems less upset, then he assumes she is asking for advice. If he assumes she is asking for advice, then he puts on his Mr. Fix-It hat to solve her problems. If he assumes she is blaming him, then he draws his sword to protect himself from attack. In both cases, he soon finds it difficult to listen.

John Gray, *Men are From Mars, Women are From Venus*

Interlude

Learning to Be Present

The affirmations in this section prepare you to become healers in your everyday interactions with those closest to you in your world. You target areas of challenge, and reprogram your minds to identify and dissolve judgmental or unloving thoughts toward others. You become aware that an unloving thought toward another creates suffering within *you*. You begin to recognize and see beyond the Pain Body in another person, providing the opening for true forgiveness and unconditional love.

Your experience of the outer world is a mirror of what lives in your own heart and mind. That is, in every interaction you have the chance to observe the extent to which your ego is in charge, and the extent to which you are allowing *Love* to work through you. We might examine every interaction with the following questions:

Am I listening? Am I hearing what this person is saying?

In the midst of conversation with someone, our mind is often drifting to something we need to take care of, planning what we're going to do after this, or distracted by myriad other thoughts. Amazing healing can take place simply by listening.

Am I prejudging what this person wants or is feeling?

In our impatience to get on to the next thing, we often decide that a person is behaving the way they behaved at some time before, or that the situation is the same as one experienced in the past. With practice, you learn to let go of preconceived ideas that limit who a person is in that moment, allowing them an opportunity to grow or think or behave in a new way.

Am I feeling superior to this person? or am I pitying this person?

In this subtle trick of the ego, we believe that we are helping someone by feeling sorry for them. With awareness, you refrain from attempting to solve the person's problem or offering advice — the greatest insult.

Am I feeling defensive? Am I feeling angry or wishing to lash out?

It may be that something in the interaction is triggering our Pain Body. You learn to see this as a blip on the screen of your mind, and choose not to react. When necessary, you may choose to remove yourself from the situation.

The answers to the above questions are an indication whether or not your True Self is Present. As you become more real in your interactions, you begin to watch your mind flip in and out of Presence many times during a conversation. At the conclusion of an encounter, you ask: *To what extent was this interaction genuine? To what extent was the interaction conditioned by the past?* You are then able to construct affirmations to undo patterned thinking in your relationships. All of your relationships, and all of your interactions, become more fulfilling as a result. Magic and mystery is born again in your life.

The realm of relationships is where your deepest inner work — the work that is transformational for the greater family of human beings — is accomplished. Every interaction that takes place with Presence brings more aliveness to your consciousness. As you offer words and thoughts that bring healing to others, at the same time you receive healing for yourself. In this way, you become an agent of healing in your world. You begin to see with Unconditional Love and experience Oneness with all of life.

Thinking You Know What's Right for Another Person

What I think is going on for another person
is only a story I concoct in my mind.

* * * * * * *

I see clearly when a situation is my business
and when it is not.

* * * * * * *

It is not my job to fix another person,
no matter who they are in relation to me.

* * * * * * *

I cannot change the thoughts or behavior of another person;
I can only change my thoughts or behavior.

* * * * * * *

I find the Truth that is there for me in every situation.

~~~~~~~~~~~~~~~~~~~~~~~~~~~~~~~~~~~~~

There are three kinds of business: Yours, mine, and God's.[1] *The psychic institute where I spent time studying taught students that if a problem doesn't go away in three days or less, then it is not your problem. In other words, it will not be fruitful for you to expend energy trying to fix the situation. This is a challenge for many of us. Absorbing ourselves with other people's stuff is one of the favorite tricks of the ego to distract us from attending to our inner work.*

---

[1]Katie, Byron. *Loving What Is.*

Wanting Someone to Change

I am irritated by [situation or habit of a person]
because I have known that situation or habit of character
in myself.

* * * * * * *

I NOW forgive myself and accept myself for
having had that habit of character.

* * * * * * *

As I am growing to release that habit of character,
so [person] is growing to understand
and release that habit.

* * * * * * *

I now allow [person] to grow through and release that
habit of character in their own way.

* * * * * * *

I let go of my condemnation or critique, as it is through my
Love and Acceptance that [person] will be stimulated
to change and grow.

---

*We've all heard the truism that we cannot change another person. But when
we step into the consciousness of our Oneness, we begin to understand that
everything we notice in another person is an aspect of our universal Self.
Everything that disturbs you is a gift for your growth, and your growing
brings growth to others.*

Wrong Thoughts or Action Toward Another Person

I recognize that my thoughts (or action) toward [person]
arose from an intention to harm or
to undermine in some way.

* * * * * * *

I recognize that my action did NOT serve [person's]
Highest Good and therefore could not serve my Own.

* * * * * * *

I forgive myself and receive the *Holy Spirit's* gift
of correction of my wrong thinking.

* * * * * * *

I NOW ask Undoing and call forth Healing
for [person] and myself.

Buddhism teaches us to be aware of the chain of Right Thought, Right Word, and Right Action. An action may appear to be kind or favorable on the surface, but if the underlying intention is not for Good, there is a thought or chain of thought in need of healing. It is possible to learn to examine your mind and take apart your thoughts until you discover the root "wrong thought." But this is not essential. An uncomfortable feeling is the only signal you need. You let go of your need to know, and your thoughts are healed simply by your desire for healing.[1]

[1] Foundation for Inner Peace. *A Course in Miracles*.

Worrying Too Much About Others

My worry thoughts are wrong expressions
of my Compassion and Love.
I give them to God, and I see [person]
surrounded by Divine Light.

* * * * * * *

I accept that my worry undermines [person's] ability
to create the experience she needs for her learning.

* * * * * * *

I let go of the idea that my worrying about potential trouble
averts a negative outcome.

* * * * * * *

I trust [person's] ability to create experiences
that clarify his understanding
of what he wishes to have more of in his life.

* * * * * * *

I help [person] by affirming the best and highest outcome
possible for all involved.

Worry is unproductive mental activity that drains the energy of both the worrier and the object of concern. The mind of a master worrier catalogs every possible disaster that could happen in a situation, trip, event, or undertaking. The fact that so many potential tragedies do not occur seems to confirm the effectiveness of the practice. This futile mental habit is the flip side of affirmative thinking.

Creating Your Own Happiness

My Happiness emanates from a wellspring deep inside of
me and is independent of conditions.

* * * * * * *

My happiness is independent of the mood of [person].

* * * * * * *

I claim my Happiness as the product of my own loving
relationship with *All That Is*.

* * * * * * *

I can experience my Happiness any time I direct my mind
to the memory of that feeling.

---

*Sensitive people, or those in caretaking roles, may come to have their energy
so enmeshed with that of another that their mood or inner state becomes
completely identified with that of the other(s). Females, especially, have
been programmed to be stoic and serve our families, setting aside our own
needs. There is satisfaction in this for a time, but at some point there is a
need to reclaim oneself and take a break from allowing others to use us as
a way to release or process their emotions. We learn to create and maintain
our own sacred internal space.*

Cultivating Noninterference

I allow [beloved person] to create his own wellbeing.
I trust that all is unfolding for him according to
the right and perfect plan for his growth and learning.

* * * * * *

I know it is not my job to fix the life of [person]
and it is not my right to try to mold or create her.

* * * * * *

I give guidance and share information when I am asked. I
encourage self-reliance when it is needed.

* * * * * *

I let go of the belief that I am responsible
for the wellbeing of [person]. I let go of the belief
that his wellbeing is dependent on what I do.

* * * * * *

I carry [beloved person] in my heart surrounded with Light
as we celebrate together
the unfolding of his Highest Good.

While it creates good karma to help others, we must stay tuned to our motivation and resist becoming too invasive or attempting to hold someone to our expectations. Here you affirm your support for the action a loved one is choosing or needing to take, even if the steps are different than you might imagine for them. You let go and invoke that the Highest Good be served.

Allowing Your Child/Spouse More Independence

Meaning in my life is derived through my own thoughts
and experiences and not through those of [person].

* * * * * * *

I accept and support [person] in choosing to have
experiences for their growth that do not include me.

* * * * * * *

I trust that [person] will seek my guidance or my
companionship in accordance with his needs.

* * * * * * *

My role in the decisions and experiences of [person] is to
encourage and appreciate.

* * * * * * *

I will know when it is right for me to involve myself in the
experiences or decisions of [person] and when it is right for
me to step back and allow.

---

*In this case, we have become so attached to a child or partner that their
need for independence throws us into intense internal struggle. We may
knowingly or unknowingly create obstacles to their pursuing the experiences
needed to grow. As mothers and wives, this is a subversion of our innate
role as nurturers. As fathers and husbands, this control behavior is an
abuse of our role as protectors and guides. As you let go and allow more
freedom, you trust your intuition to alert you to a situation where your
action or intervention is called for.*

Improving Communication

The channel of communication between me and [person]
is cleansed and strengthened.

* * * * * * *

Each of us is empowered to safely share our Truth as we
discuss and explore this problem
[decision, relationship etc.].

* * * * * * *

Each of us sets aside old ideas about the other,
the relationship, and the dimensions of the problem.

* * * * * * *

We are brought together at the perfect time when our
hearts and minds are open.

* * * * * * *

As we share our Truth, this problem dissolves and
transforms into Growth.

---

*This set of statements, and those on the next two pages, focus on embracing
new and better skills for communicating our needs in a way that does
not make the other person wrong. At the same time, we must be true to
ourselves and learn to express whatever discomfort we are feeling, rather
than suppressing it.*[1]

---

[1] Rosenberg, Marshall. *Nonviolent Communication.*

Expressing Your Feelings and Needs

The energy is set for [person] and myself to communicate in
a deeply meaningful way.

* * * * * *

I let go of fixed ideas about what needs to change
or what needs to happen to make me feel better.

* * * * * *

I express the Truth of how I feel about [situation] in a way
that does not blame or shame.

* * * * * *

By expressing ourselves openly, both parties
are empowered to exchange what is alive in us
in a way that deepens our humanness.

* * * * * *

This communication creates new ideas both for myself and
[person] for going forward.

Hurtful Behavior from Someone
You Care About

I fearlessly explore the nature of my connection to [person]
as a trigger for this feeling of hurt or anger.

* * * * * * *

I experience this anger [or hurt] because a memory from
the past has awakened. I have temporarily forgotten
the Magnificent Being that I Am.

* * * * * * *

[Person's] insensitivity is a reflection
of the deep pain within him/her.
My heart opens with compassion for [person].

* * * * * * *

Hurtful words and behavior flow through me
like an arrow made of jello
melting into the deep pool of *God's Love*.

* * * * * * *

I grow within myself and in
my relationship with [person].

* * * * * * *

I respond to insensitive messages in a lighthearted way
that undoes and redirects the energy into healing
for [person] and for myself.

Getting Free of Parental Disapproval

I am grateful to my parents for the love and comfort they
have provided me in this lifetime.

* * * * * * *

I can honor my parents and still live my Truth.

* * * * * * *

I am grateful to my parents for giving birth to me, but it is I
who create and decide Who I Am in this moment.

* * * * * * *

My parents' disapproval mirrors their history, from which
I explore and glean the lesson that is there for me.

* * * * * * *

My parents made the best decisions they could,
given the conditions of their lives
and the information available to them.

* * * * * * *

I grow and change and become the person I am inside
even if my parents are not able to appreciate my choices.

~~~~~~

*I was 50 years old when I released the need for my parents to see and
appreciate something of my deeper self. Now I am no longer affected by
my mother's disapproving once-over of my clothes and hair. I recognize
when my dad's Pain Body is activated, and I attempt to deflect or refocus
his complaints. Often, when my dad is speaking from his real self, he asks
for prayer.*

Needing Someone's Approval — Facing Criticism or Disapproval (commentary)

~~~~~~~~~~~~~~~~~~~~~~~~~~~~~~~~~~~~

In order for us to express our gifts fully in this lifetime, we must be "independent of the good opinion of others." At the same time, paying attention to how we are perceived by others helps us to refine ourselves and become more of the person we truly wish to be.[1]

---

[1] Dyer, Wayne. *The Power of Intention.*

Needing Someone's Approval — Facing Criticism or Disapproval

I turn inward to find my direction and my self-worth.

* * * * * * *

My inner voice guides me toward expressing more and
more of Who I Really Am.

* * * * * * *

I let go of relying on validation from others to determine
the worth of my thoughts, plans, or pursuits.

* * * * * * *

I let go of the need to be thought of as a "good person"
or a "nice person."

* * * * * * *

Criticism or disapproval from others cannot deter me
from expressing Who I Really Am.

* * * * * * *

I bless those who disapprove of or criticize me and cherish
the learning that this experience holds for me.

* * * * * * *

I explore and embrace criticism either as a sign I am going
in the right direction, or a signal that leads me
to adjust something for the better.

Healing Estrangement (commentary)

~~~~~~~~~~~~~~~~~~~~~~~~~~~~~~~~~~~~~~

After years of a negative pattern of interaction with a person that produces unpleasant after-effects, we may believe there is no reconciliation possible with that person. We attempt to obliterate them in our soul memory, but the more we try to do this, the more it seems we are drawn to this person.

One of the participants in our Course In Miracles *study group recounted a feeling of uneasiness knowing that he would soon be visiting with his sister and her family. Past visits had been unpleasant due to his sister's adherence to traditional Christian viewpoints that he perceived were unreceptive or critical of his chosen path. After the group helped him to see with new eyes, he determined to enter into the next visit with a heart and mind seeking only to appreciate his sister and her family, and the unique relationship they shared as brother and sister. Upon his return, he described with choked emotion the wonderful visit he had and the seemingly magical things that occurred between all members of the family.*

Although it is hard to accept, probably every one of us knows someone who is estranged from or in a difficult relationship with a parent, or who is a parent estranged from their grown children. A cycle of negatively charged interactions plays out as both parties continue to add to their list of grievances against the other. Conscious awareness of this pattern and a clear intention to change it through love and acceptance leads to miraculous results.

Healing Estrangement (Yourself and Another Person)

Whatever occurred to close my heart to [person] and to
close his/her heart to me is erased from memory.

* * * * * * *

A new relationship between me and [person]
is born in this moment.

* * * * * * *

I bless [person] and wish him/her only Good.

* * * * * * *

I do not have to take any action, and trust that
our communication is rekindled in a miraculous way.

Healing Estrangement Between Two Persons

A thread of Love and Forgiveness arises
as rainbow light within the field of grey
between [name of two persons].

* * * * * * *

The memory of their history vanishes in a moment and
they meet again, with Generosity.

* * * * * * *

They meet again as if for the first time, with Joy.

Getting Beyond Grudges

I know that [painful incident(s) from the past with
person(s)] took place so that I might learn and grow.

* * * * * * *

I forgive [person(s)], knowing that they behaved in the
best way they could in accordance with
the understanding they had at the time.

* * * * * * *

I forgive myself for my role in this experience, knowing that
I behaved in the best way I could at the time.

* * * * * * *

I NOW receive the learning this experience holds for me.
I NOW transform this memory and store it differently
in my consciousness because the
learning I need is complete.

* * * * * * *

I am open to a shift in the energy between [person] and
myself. I experience a feeling of loving acceptance
as I imagine the face of [person].

* * * * * * *

This freedom lightens my heart and fills me with Joy.

---

*A grudge is the result of repeated negative experiences with a person, leading
you to store a fixed idea or belief about them in your mind. Even if this
person is no longer in your life, transforming a deeply held negative belief
brings healing for all parties involved.*

Loneliness — Wanting More Attention from Spouse or Lover (commentary)

~~~~~~

There are many potential causes for loss of sexual passion in a love relationship. Regardless of the cause, the couple moves to higher ground if they are willing to communicate and respond to feelings and needs. One of the partners may temporarily need more distance as he or she is working through old thoughts or habits that have surfaced as a result of their inner work. Or, the dynamics of the relationship may have changed due to the involvement of a new person in their lives (e.g., a child returns from college; a friend moves in for a time).

In a love relationship, the experience of intimacy as companionship and sexual intimacy are closely linked. The couple may have reached the limit of their knowledge either of the physical or the emotional dimension. Sometimes, the sexual problem is a relationship problem that can be helped by becoming better partners and learning to be more open with each other.[1]

The affirmations included here open the way for real communication to take place between the partners. No matter what the situation brings, it is important to remember that love between two persons is but a reflection of the experience of limitless and unchanging Love that is always available to us.

---

[1]Kasl, Charlotte. *If the Buddha Married.*

135

Loneliness — Wanting More Attention from Spouse or Lover

I accept that times of intense closeness and times of
relative separateness are part of the natural vibration
of a love relationship.

* * * * * *

These feelings of loneliness and discontent are a vehicle
for moving to a higher level of communication and trust.

* * * * * *

The right opportunity arises for me to share my feelings
and needs with my partner. I welcome hearing
my partner's feelings and needs.

* * * * * *

I accept my role in creating habit patterns that led to a lack
of connectivity between us.

* * * * * *

Lack of passion between my lover and myself does not
impact the truth of myself as a loving person, whole and
perfect in every way, loved by *All That IS*.

* * * * * *

In acknowledging the lack of closeness and passion
between us, we open to understanding and receiving
the messages that are there for us.

* * * * * * *

I open to the *Infinite Love of the Divine Spirit,* inviting this *Holy Energy* to fill every emptiness or void within me.

* * * * * * *

My partner and I explore ideas that help us break through old patterns to discover renewed enthusiasm.

Loving and Letting Go

In the eyes of my beloved, I behold the Love of the Universe,
the *Supreme Passion*.

* * * * * * *

I expand my heart with this feeling of Love, glorifying its
eternal nature, offering it to *God*.

* * * * * * *

Expanding with this feeling, I experience the passion
felt by the *Universal Love Energy* for every one of us.

* * * * * * *

This feeling awakens me to express more Love toward
everything I see and everyone I encounter.

* * * * * * *

I rest within the embrace of the *Divine Spirit*, as it is there my
passion finds a home.

Love is experienced as painful when we hold expectations for the future that cannot be met. He loves you, but has to move away. You and she enjoy many blissful rendezvous, but you realize she has no intention of leaving her marriage or disrupting her family life. Or perhaps the two of you developed special feeling for one another during a project that is soon to be completed. Here we bless and sanctify this emotion, dedicating it to the place where all Love resides, eternally, surrounded by the Grace of the Infinite.

CHAPTER SEVEN

SHINING THROUGH
THE BIG STUFF

Love is everything. It is the energy of the Universe. It is the divine, unseen, unifying force that holds everything together. It is in us, around us, and connects us. Love belongs to everyone and everything; there are no boundaries, belief systems, religious or political ideology, or prejudice that can control or manipulate love. It is the only real thing that exists, and each of us is made of it.

James Van Praagh, *Healing Grief*

Interlude

Creating Affirmations to Help Other People

Perhaps the most difficult situations are those where someone you love appears to be suffering with a problem or challenge. Often, when hearing the story of a friend or family member's tough situation, you are pulled into their (often temporary) self-doubt and may succumb to worry or fear on their behalf.

This is not a constructive response, as the energy of fear thoughts is registered in the *Universal Mind* in a way that contributes to the person's lack of belief in his or her ability to solve the problem. As the feeling of worry inside you is not a comfortable one, your urge is to take action in some way because it makes *you* feel better, whether or not it helps the other person. There are times, of course, when constructive action on your part is called for, and in those cases you depend on receiving a clear message of how to help.

But in fact, most problems faced by a person are something they have become involved in (attracted through their thought — even if unintentionally) for the purpose of their learning. It is through creating "situations of contrast" that we humans clarify and learn to choose what it is we want and thus direct our thoughts in a new way.[1]

This learning may be as simple as "I'm not going to do that again!" but nonetheless it's important for the lesson to be absorbed into the fabric of a person's being. It is important to resist taking action that will interfere with the person's learning experience or that will complicate the situation in the long run. Offering an affirmation is an alternative way for you to support the person in their process while allowing them to own and solve their problem.

Affirmations are a way of taking non-interfering action that is of benefit to another person's life process. In the affirmation, you offer a picture of wellbeing for the other person, leaving it to them to apply that thought to the extent they choose to, or have the capability. An affirmation may be presented to a person with instructions on how to utilize it, or in the case of someone who is resistant to these ideas or, for another reason, is unable to receive the offering, holding the affirmation on their behalf will accomplish the same purpose.

Every person is an active thought creator just as you are, having equal access to the universal pool of thought, so the energy of your offering will be received by them. Affirmations offered for others help those who you care about by offering a message of wellbeing into the field of consciousness where it can be utilized by those you love for sustenance and growth.

---

[1] Hicks, Esther and Jerry (Teachings of Abraham). *The Amazing Power of Deliberate Intent.*

Creating a Love Relationship

I am worthy and capable of giving Love and receiving Love.
I am open to right and perfect partnership NOW.

* * * * * * *

I am willing to understand what it takes to have true
partnership. I trust that the steps I need to go through
will be revealed to me.

* * * * * * *

I bless and acknowledge my past experiences for bringing
me readiness for this new and deeper experience of Love.

* * * * * * *

I release old definitions of who I think I am
based on past hurt or victim experiences.
I NOW attract my perfect partner.

This affirmation begins the process of creating an opening for
someone new to enter into your life. In conjunction with the use of
statements such as these, try creating a vision statement for your
perfect partnership. Read your vision statement frequently and
return to it in your thoughts. Focus on how you want to feel when
you are with this person; see the two of you sharing activities you
love. Hold these pictures in your mind, rather than specific features
of what he or she looks like or the job they have. Believe and you
shall receive!

Manifesting Your Dream Home

We open to the process of exploration and
inner negotiation to manifest our dream home.

* * * * * * *

We NOW propose to the Source our highest imagination
of the home we want, providing feedback
to the Universe on the possibilities that result.

* * * * * * *

We hone our vision and allow it to incrementally grow.

* * * * * * *

The right and perfect property with features matching that
of our highest imagination,
with the right and perfect price and terms,
manifests for us at the right and perfect time.

---

*In finding our property, my husband and I first defined the bottom line
features of our dream place: near water; includes a rental; reasonable
commute distance for both of us. This was modified to include garden space
as big as what we currently enjoyed, or better; and a place for the dog to run
as big as what he had or larger. As we visited more properties, we added
sunlight, and being close to amenities. We imagined what it would feel
like to be in our new place, what we wanted to create together. Once we
had clarity on these things, the moment we stepped onto the property we
now own, we turned to one another and said simultaneously "This is it!"*

Creating Your Right Work

I know that *God* is the Source of my Supply.

* * * * * * *

I accept Abundance as my birthright and Prosperity
as my natural state of being.

* * * * * * *

My physical and emotional needs are met beyond my
wildest expectations as I open myself to
receiving assistance from the Divine.

* * * * * * *

I NOW choose to follow the path of my heart,
knowing that everything I need for my happiness
has already been provided.

* * * * * * *

I give thanks for the chance to awaken to this Truth.
I NOW forgive and let go of any wrong thinking.
I NOW call forth that which delights my Soul.

This is the time to look deep within yourself to identify the desires of your heart. At the same time, you identify and undo the limiting thoughts programmed into your mind — that you are not good enough, that you will fail at what you try. You must be prepared to revise your plan as you go along. When you embrace the joy of the process, you experience the true meaning of creation.

Caring for Aging Parents

I gracefully transition into my new role as caregiver
or decision-maker for Mom and Dad.

* * * * * * *

I set aside all resentment and set my intention on Good,
knowing that only Good can be the result.

* * * * * * *

In caring for my Mom and Dad, I give back to the Universe
the Love that has been given to me.

* * * * * * *

I trust myself to make decisions that serve the
Highest Good for Mom and Dad, even if they are unable
to understand or show appreciation.

* * * * * * *

I do the best I can with what is in front of me. I rely on *God*
to handle what I cannot see or understand.
Help comes in unexpected and surprising ways.

---

*Navigating the dynamics of decision-making for the care for one's aging
parents brings even the most stalwart atheist to call for divine assistance.
"I've decided it's a puzzle," my sister said, "and I'm not smart enough to
figure it out." When we open ourselves to Higher Direction, our Spirit
Guides jump in with joy and we are overwhelmed by miracles.*

Moving

All plans and arrangements for the move to my new home
are accomplished easily and in perfect timing.

* * * * * * *

We make easy decisions about what we want to purge,
donate, or move to our new home.

* * * * * * *

The energy of every experience of Joy in the home
I am leaving surrounds me in my new home.

* * * * * * *

The energy of every experience of Sorrow in the home we
are leaving is blessed and absorbed into the *Infinite* where
it is healed and removed from memory.

* * * * * * *

All energy of former occupants in my new home
is blessed and cleared for my arrival.

* * * * * * *

I embrace the welcoming energy of my new home
as it embraces me.

*Use of rituals for property blessing help you to detach from the former
home, set the energy in the new space, and prepare yourself for the change.
Where the move is a group experience, affirmations help unify everyone
involved and allow an opportunity to allay fears.*

Accidents (commentary)

It is often said, "Be careful what you wish for, you might get it." As you expand your level of consciousness, this becomes closer to "Be careful what you wish for, you WILL get it." When I wanted to unload myself from my SUV and the loan that went with it, the car was totaled by a construction vehicle while parked on the street. I was shocked, but later was amazed at how the event served my needs.

Accidents may be the playing out of karmic agreements. A visitor to our Unity church asked me how it could happen that a friend, a minister, who crossed the highway to help someone whose car had broken down was hit by a car and killed. I attempted words of consolation. Perhaps he had fulfilled his work here and was ready to move on to his next assignment. Perhaps he had asked for a quick transition. We cannot know why something happens to another person. When it happens to you, you give in to the possibility that a greater purpose has been served, and when your heart is open, you receive an answer you can live with. Then you let it go and move on.

Accidents

Although the occurrence of [accident] may appear to be random or unfair or without explanation, I KNOW that my experience of [accident] contributes in some way to my Greater Good or that of someone with whom I have agreed to play a part.

* * * * * * *

I accept that all lessons from my experience of [accident] have been received.

* * * * * * *

I trust that the higher purpose served by [accident] is revealed to me at the right time.

Menopause (commentary)

~~~~~~

How lovely it would be to support our sisters going through menopause by encircling them to guard their rest and comforting them with rituals of transformation. Instead, we view this natural transition as a problem or sickness that requires a pharmaceutical solution. My sister said to me, "You had an easy time, so you can't understand the misery of hot flashes, dizziness, and insomnia." I had all those symptoms — but somehow I welcomed each new stage as bringing me closer to freedom from monthly cycles, and this was foremost in my mind. Menopause also coincided with my kids finishing high school and going on to college, so suddenly I was my own person. I also decided this was the time to break free from my Mother's opinion of me — I grew my hair long, redecorated my house, and bought clothes that I always wanted to wear. Oh — and I got divorced too!

Menopause

I am ecstatic to NOW become the person
I came into this life to be.

* * * * * * *

I embrace the awesome freedom from monthly cycles that
kept me trapped and limited.

* * * * * * *

Information and assistance with this transition
comes to me in amazing ways at the exact time
and manner that I am able to receive it.

* * * * * * *

I embrace the path to my freedom and travel through
momentary discomfort with ease.

* * * * * * *

I NOW become the Wise Woman,
Heaven's Mistress, fit and free as a bird.

Illness (Your Own)

The Infinite Energy which is God brings me to understand
the purpose of my experience of [illness].

* * * * * * *

I AM God's perfect child. Every experience expands my
understanding of God's Love in my life.

* * * * * * *

My mind is at perfect peace today. I am safe in the world
today. Every thought I have affirms this.

* * * * * * *

Only Love is real. Only that which emanates
from LOVE can be present in my experience.

* * * * * * *

My mind and body are clear, refreshed, and open to
receiving new information about the Universe
and my part in it.

---

*The biggest challenge when faced with serious illness is to continue in
our faith and not fall into fear. The experience of an illness is unique
and individual, bringing us face to face with our deepest obstacles. The
meaning is often more complex than we can grasp with the logical mind.
We continue to affirm that all is well, and allow healing to take place on
another plane of consciousness.*

Illness of Friend or Family Member

This condition of illness in [family member or friend]
is necessary for their growth as a Spirit and also
for my own growth in relationship with them.

* * * * * * *

I allow [person] to experience [condition or illness]
in the way that is most conducive to their receiving
the healing they are seeking.

* * * * * * *

I open my heart to Guidance on the role I am invited
to play in the healing lessons of [person].

* * * * * * *

I remain solidly grounded in my own wellbeing.
I receive Higher Guidance in every moment
as I stand strong in service.

* * * * * * *

My resistance and fear is transformed in the NOW
of this experience.

*Friends and loved ones find new courage when we envision them well
and whole, in perfect health. We affirm that all is happening in the right
and perfect way, no matter how things appear. The strength of our belief
creates trust within the sick person, helping them to move through and
beyond the time of challenge.*

Death of Beloved Person
or Animal Companion

I say hello to the Soul of [name of person or animal friend],
knowing my greeting is received.

* * * * * * *

I offer all thoughts of things not said or done in the time
of our relationship to *God* for healing.

* * * * * * *

All things that should have been said, and all things that
should have been done are now completed
outside of the boundaries of time.

* * * * * * *

The crossing of this friend into the Beyond creates a link
for me with *the Infinite* as I continue in this life.

* * * * * * *

I give my grief to *God* and open my heart to healing.

* * * * * * *

I am blessed with fond recollections that sustain me
through this sorrow.

---

*A set of affirmative statements can in no way address the energy adjustment
that occurs hand in hand with the momentous occasion of a loved one's
passing. What is important here is to recognize the enormity of what has
occurred, and allow — and yes! even embrace — the unfolding of the
grieving process.*[1]

---

[1] Fumia, Molly. *Safe Passage.*

CHAPTER EIGHT

THRIVING AT WORK

The key to a successful career is realizing that it's not separate from the rest of your life, but is rather an extension of your most basic self. And your most basic self is love.

Marianne Williamson, *A Return to Love*

An internal tolerance of stress undermines the initiative to uncover its source and change behaviors and systems to relieve the pressure. When, however, relaxation becomes our real standard, it creates a deep need for the resolution of dissonance, which is the core dynamic of productivity. We make things happen to relieve the creative discomfort of things undone.

David Allen, *Getting Things Done*

Interlude

Staying True to Yourself Out in the World

Many of us may have understood work as necessary to provide for our basic survival, for building our self-esteem, and as a means for ensuring security in our old age. We have understood that the world of work can involve struggle and competition, often within hierarchical structures where we are subject to the whims of others who have power over us. Many of us have made the mistake of letting our work define who we think we are, falling into confusion or depression when our job changes, we lose our job, or we retire.

But when you open to the true meaning of work, you see that work is a way to invoke and participate in the flow of abundance in our world. You express your gifts and talents, experiencing the reward of abundance and gratitude. No matter whether you are in business for yourself, or work for a company or enterprise, work is a wonderful vehicle to explore interaction and interdependence with others outside of your home and family.

When we perform an action, the invisible within us finds a form and comes to expression. Therefore, our work should be the place where the soul can enjoy becoming visible and present. The rich unknown, reserved and precious within us, can emerge into visible form. Our nature longs deeply for the possibility of expression in what we call work.[1]

One of the most liberating aspects of your evolving Consciousness is a shift in your point of view regarding work. As you open to co-creating with Spirit, all your interactions in the world are embraced as opportunities to act with more awareness, behaving in a way that is more true to yourself, while at the same time honoring others.

As you learn to live your life *from the inside out*, rather than believing you are subject to the world acting upon you, you respond with more aliveness and an ability to behave genuinely in the moment.

You are aware of the character or personality of individuals. But, as you awaken, you become aware that companies, and teams within companies, also have personalities. This is true for all levels of organizations — of families, cities and towns, nations. When you are able to broaden your abilities of perception, the boundaries of your personhood begin to blur. On the quantum level, the desires and intentions of all involved in an enterprise interact in the Field of Pure Potentiality. In this way, affirmations coming from the heart — whether directed at yourself, other individuals, or groups within an organization — have power to affect positive change.

This chapter and the one that follows include affirmations designed to support the individual at work — to become better organized, more effective, to be appreciated — as well as affirmations directed toward shifting the energy around other persons, teams, or management within the organization to further overall goals. As it is not possible for an ordinary personality to completely see what outcome is most beneficial, the affirmations are worded so as to invite the highest good for all involved. As you practice with affirmations and study the power of your thoughts, you come to know that the power of an affirmation increases in accordance with the purity of the intention behind it.

> *Dear God, please give my life some sense of purpose. Use me as an instrument of your peace. Use my talents and abilities to spread love. I surrender my job to you. Help me to remember that my real job is to love the world back to health. Thank you very much.*[2]

---

[1]O'Donohue, John. *Anam Cara*, p. 134.
[2]Williamson, Marianne, *A Return to Love*, p. 157.

Being in the Flow in Your Job

I am skillful, effective, and filled with boundless energy.

* * * * * * *

I am surrounded by joyful, capable people. There is a feeling of camaraderie in my workplace.

* * * * * * *

I make a valuable contribution to the project [or team].

* * * * * * *

Next steps and tasks to accomplish both immediate and long-term objectives are revealed to me.

* * * * * * *

Assistance comes in ways that surprise and delight me.

* * * * * * *

I navigate difficult situations with ease and finesse.

* * * * * * *

I treat others with kindness and respect no matter what challenges I may be facing in the moment.

* * * * * * *

I have more than enough time to accomplish everything I need to do.

Whether your work satisfies you at the deepest level of your soul, or is a bridge to that which fulfills your soul's purpose, embracing where you are right now brings growth and reward.

Leadership

The motivation of the leader(s) is to serve the best and
highest good for all involved in the enterprise.

* * * * * * *

The leaders create a unified vision for success and
plan together how to achieve goals and objectives.

* * * * * * *

The leaders have all the information and resources
they need to achieve the mission of the company
[business/organization/group/project].

* * * * * * *

All necessary conditions are in place to attract new and
capable leadership that is an energetic match
for this company's goals and mission.

---

*Leaders must have the highest personal integrity. They need to coordinate
amongst themselves, and assure adequate resources to accomplish the goals.
Sometimes, they need to know when it is time to move on. Most workers do
not realize that the personalities of the leaders and the associated dynamics
of the group or organization contribute more to their liking or hating their
job than the specifics of their job description or even how much they get
paid. Companies and groups within companies acquire personalities that
reflect the character of their leader. Thus, offering affirmations on behalf
of leaders has a direct payoff for everyone in the organization.*

Being Organized and Productive

I joyfully create time each week to write down
and organize all of the tasks, goals, and concerns
of both my home and work life.

* * * * * * *

I create time each week to organize and file
the paperwork on my desk.

* * * * * * *

I regularly review progress to reestablish
timelines and next steps.

* * * * * * *

Methods, materials, and other solutions for becoming and
staying organized are brought to my attention
as needed.

In our brains, home life tasks/goals and work life tasks/goals are intertwined. In a "mind dump" process, you write every thought and concern in your mind down on paper. You then organize these random concerns into lists according to type of task and effort required. This action frees your mind to engage in the creative thinking you are unable to do when your message center is occupied keeping track of the "hanging loops" in your brain.[1] Clearing of your mind also opens you to receiving divine assistance through your affirmations!

---

[1]Allen, Richard. *Getting Things Done: The Art of Stress-Free Productivity.*

Communicating Your Needs/Requests

I communicate my need for [higher salary, more staff
support etc.] to leadership at the right time
and in the right way.

* * * * * *

I communicate my needs and requests in a way that shows
my appreciation of the greater mission
of the organization or team.

* * * * * *

The leadership responds positively to my requests.

Being Rewarded for Your Talents

I dedicate my endeavors to bringing the highest benefit for
all involved.

* * * * * *

My gifts and talents bring me abundant reward.

* * * * * *

My salary increases to an extent I had not
imagined possible.

* * * * * *

I am grateful for the ease with which things happen
in my life to increase my Good.

Making Friends with Technology

My computer [or other tool] is my ally in all that I do
and accomplish.

* * * * * * *

I welcome advances in technology. I enthusiastically seek
expert assistance when needed.

* * * * * * *

Patterns experienced by my hands and eyes are imprinted
in my subconscious mind and easily recalled.

* * * * * * *

I match my thought pattern with that of a new program
and I learn quickly.

* * * * * * *

I am grateful for this ability to extend my consciousness
and connect to the world through my computer.

It requires a certain flexibility of thought to keep up with the constant changes in technology. Certain people seem to attract computer problems, while others experience only rare or minor irritations. The computer is an extension of the human brain. Because a microchip translates and transmits energy, computers absorb and respond to the energy of the user. You get in the flow of your world when you sustain an attitude of gratitude toward your machines in the same way you do toward all the other blessings in your life.

Meeting a Deadline

I focus my mind and body on accomplishing
[this project or task].

* * * * * * *

The steps I must take to accomplish the task are clear.

* * * * * * *

I easily set aside competing priorities
and am not distracted by them.

* * * * * * *

Success is the grand picture in my mind
and my efforts are appreciated.

An inner lack of confidence in your own abilities, or a belief that the outcome will be less than satisfying to yourself or to those who have requested the project, can deter you from entering into and completing a task with your full attention and talent. It is important to set your mind to look forward to your own satisfaction at your achievement, knowing that it is worthy. It is the projection of your own thought that sets up how your work is received by others, even more than the absolute quality of the product as measured by some imaginary scale.

Writing a Report — Preparing a Presentation

I easily envision the structure and content of this report
[or presentation].

* * * * * * *

I envision and structure my day with adequate time
to accomplish [writing project].

* * * * * * *

The perfect conditions for focus and concentration
arise at the perfect time.

* * * * * * *

Setting down the first few lines, my mind is focused 100%
on the project and the rest flows easily.

* * * * * * *

I am free of interruptions and accomplish the project
in the time I allotted for it.

Business Travel

My travel is efficient and uneventful. I am rested
and have comfortable accommodations.

* * * * * * *

I partake of nourishing meals with pleasant company.

* * * * * * *

I am well organized and have everything I need.
Mechanical devices operate with precision and flow.

* * * * * * *

Interactions take place as planned and my goals
are easily accomplished.

Cooperation and Team-Building

The leadership effectively communicates
a short term and long range vision
that guides day to day decision-making.

* * * * * * *

The members of our team [organization]
are supportive of one another.

* * * * * * *

The members of our team trust one another.

* * * * * * *

The members of our team collaborate with one another
for planning and executing projects.

* * * * * * *

All members of the team are given credit for successes.

* * * * * * *

Members of our team speak highly of one another
to other co-workers.

* * * * * * *

Our team handles problems or misunderstandings
by talking things through together.

~~~~~~~~~~~~~~~~~~~~~~~~~~~~~~~~~~~~~~

*Teams are the foundation of all work. Cooperation and networking are the
basis for success in the paradigm of greater consciousness.*

Securing Grants and Funding

My work contributes in fundamental and key ways
to the advancement of knowledge in my field.

* * * * * *

I am successful at identifying sources of grants and funding
that match the project goals.

* * * * * *

I easily collect the necessary information and obtain
buy-in from essential persons to support my
grant application.

* * * * * *

I create time to focus my energy on grant writing and
easily submit the application by the deadline.

* * * * * *

I honor and give thanks for my grant funds as a gift from
the Universe and maintain the highest level
of integrity in my work.

Making Useful Contacts

I draw to myself the right and perfect people who assist me
in accomplishing [this task or goal].

Adequate Staffing and Budget

Our group [organization] receives sufficient staffing
and budget to achieve its goals and objectives.

* * * * * * *

The leaders refine the goals and objectives
to be consistent with the staffing and budget available.

Workspace

The leaders allocate space and resources so as to achieve
the Highest Good for the organization as a whole.

* * * * * * *

The workspace of our group [my workspace] is
well-equipped, comfortable, and conducive to the
highest productivity.

* * * * * * *

I and my team are outfitted with the latest technological
solutions, creating high morale within the group.

---

*Sometimes more resources and staffing are needed. More often we need
to rethink our expectations, given the resources and staffing available.
Space is a common battleground in organizations. Here you affirm that
the leadership holds a vision for the highest good of the whole, rather than
responding to the loudest voice or rewarding a pet project.*

Contributing to Meetings

I am motivated by the best and highest good for the
organization as a whole.

* * * * * * *

I provide information based on my years of experience to
support decision-making at this meeting.

* * * * * * *

I express myself clearly and succinctly, providing a sound
rationale for my viewpoint.

* * * * * * *

Others recognize my purity of intention and integrity,
whether or not they agree with me.

Meeting Dynamics

Every person in the room feels empowered
to express his or her ideas, and respects the ideas
of every other person.

* * * * * * *

There is dynamic and stimulating interaction.
Consensus is reached on next steps.

* * * * * * *

The participants feel their time was well spent
and the meeting was meaningful and valuable.

Effective Committee Chair

The Chair creates operating procedures that clearly define
the domains and activity of the committee.

* * * * * * *

The Chair receives the help of key team members who
contribute to establishing the agendas.

* * * * * * *

The Chair creates time to review the agenda items, gather
materials, and envision how the meeting will go.

* * * * * * *

The Chair sequences the topics to make the best use of
key people's time and energy.

* * * * * * *

The Chair encourages everyone present to contribute
his or her ideas and information.

* * * * * * *

The Chair offers coherent summations of the information
provided vis a vis the task at hand.

* * * * * * *

The Chair brings discussion of agenda items to a close
or resolution at the right time and in the right way.

---

*The style of the chair sets the energy for the committee, and styles are as
varied as individuals. These affirmative statements invoke Divine assistance
to improve the Chair, rather than wasting your energy criticizing (which
is so tempting to do).*

Investments and Retirement

I can handle risk and approach my investing
with a sense of adventure.

* * * * * * *

I make time to learn about investing and
always make good choices.

* * * * * * *

My investments yield growth
beyond my wildest expectations.

* * * * * * *

I intuit when to ride out a tough period
and when to change strategy.

* * * * * * *

I envision my retirement and the steps to achieve it.

* * * * * * *

The steps to achieving my retirement goals unfold
in the perfect way with perfect timing.

* * * * * * *

My investments are more than adequate
to see to my retirement needs.

CHAPTER NINE

TRANSCENDING WORKPLACE CHALLENGES

Always you have been told that work is a curse and labour a misfortune. But I say to you that when you work you fulfill a part of earth's furthest dream, assigned to you when that dream was born, and in keeping yourself with labour, you are in truth loving life, and to love life through labour is to be intimate with life's inmost secret.

Kahlil Gibran, *The Prophet*

Interlude

Keeping Balance Through Unstable Times

Organizations and teams within an organization operate as communities of individuals, and in a complex way come to express a group personality or character. Some companies, groups, or teams are harmonious and operate with an intention to create greater good in the world. Others place profit as the highest motive and behave with ruthless disregard for the impact of decisions on the greater human family.

Within a team or organization, there may be conflict between the individual members, just as there can be conflict between the multiple ego-selves inhabiting our own minds. Certain work groups or companies become known as trustworthy and dependable. These groups are understood to have *integrity*, in the same way we might characterize an individual. Such groups and individuals are viewed with a great deal of trust by other groups and organizations.

In the modern workplace, a negative atmosphere can be very destructive. When we speak of an individual, we speak of his presence. Presence is the way a person's individuality comes toward you. . . When we speak of this presence in relation to a group of people, we refer to it as atmosphere or ethos. The ethos of a workplace is a very subtle group presence. It is difficult to describe or analyze an ethos; yet you immediately sense its power and effect. Where the ethos is positive, wonderful things can happen. It is a joy to come to work because the atmosphere comes out to meet you, and it is caring, kind, and creative. If the ethos of the workplace is negative and destructive, then when people wake up in the morning, their first thought of going to work literally makes them ill. The workplace can be quite hostile; and it is often an environment of power. ... This is not a welcoming atmosphere.[1]

In a work environment, you sometimes find yourself feeling unhappy, frustrated or powerless. As your self-awareness grows, you begin to be able to discern the ethos or energy of the group or team with which you work. You recognize that this group energy — how comfortable things feel, how easily tasks flow — also fluctuates from day to day depending on your own mood interacting with that of others, at the same time influenced by planetary energies.

You learn to read the energy and know when to move something forward, or when to hold back and wait. You know when to approach a powerful person, or when to keep your distance. In sensitive situations, rather than provoking or confronting someone, you can employ affirmations to shift the energy of individuals or teams on behalf of the good of the whole.

An important part of your practice is learning to disengage yourself from ego-identification with your job. While a sense of belonging is a basic human need, it is possible to participate fully in your work while at the same time practicing non-attachment. That is, you maintain awareness of the degree to which you are deriving your identity through your work, and use affirmations to maintain inner balance and autonomy of mind.

---

[1]O'Donohue, John. *Anam Cara.*

Tolerating Fluctuations and Ambiguity

I accept that times of instability or decay
are part of the natural cycle of existence.

* * * * * * *

I accept that there are times when no action is fruitful
and I allow what is in motion to play out.

* * * * * * *

I remain steadfast within myself
no matter what external circumstances bring.

* * * * * * *

I see to the needs of my team and the organization
day to day in the best way I can.

* * * * * * *

I am patient through this period of flux, knowing I will see
the way clearly when the time is right.

All energy naturally cycles through periods of rising (coalescing) and falling (fragmentation). Having tuned in to the creative power of your thoughts, you are able to maintain the broader perspective. You free yourself of reliance on external symbols and roles, such as your job, to define who you are. You do your best to help those who are fearful. You ride it out, no matter what is taking place, confident you will know if and when action is called for on your part. You are sustained by the Universe no matter what circumstances bring.

Overcoming Inertia or Obstacles (commentary)

Initially, you accept the possibility that you are the obstacle and clear your ego involvement in what you are trying to do. Another possibility is that an unproductive energy cycle is in play either within your organization or resulting from an interaction of larger planetary forces. Through turning inward and letting go, you stop trying to force things and offer the problem out for higher guidance (the Divine is the best and cheapest consultant you can ever have!). When you are centered, you trust your inner voice or feeling to let you know when and what kind of action to take, or when to sit back and wait. You intuit when a colleague will be receptive to an entreaty for help. You experience clarity and direction when it is time to rethink what you are proposing or the players involved.

Overcoming Inertia or Obstacles

I clear myself of the desire for personal achievement
or reward and put the goals of the group first.

* * * * * * *

I step back and allow the messages inherent in the
obstacles that have arisen to reveal themselves to me.

* * * * * * *

I know when to hold off and wait for conditions
to become more favorable.

* * * * * * *

I am open to rethinking this project or the players involved
in light of the difficulties in moving it forward.

* * * * * * *

I approach key persons at the right time
and in the right way to release the inertia
and overcome the obstacles.

Feeling of Not Measuring Up to Expectations (commentary)

~~~~~~~~~~~~~~~~~~~~~~~~~~~~~~~~~~~~~

What is most important is to first accept the situation, resisting the tendency to either affix blame onto someone, or to trash yourself for your inadequacy. Whether you are falling short of your own expectations, or those of your managers or compatriots, this feeling may be indicative of a mismatch between the conditions of the job and the conditions needed for you to thrive. If you feel this is the work situation of your heart, you affirm that a shift in the energy occurs that returns your comfort. Alternatively, it may be time for you to begin visioning where your desires are leading you.

Feeling of Not Measuring Up to Expectations

These feelings of not functioning well in my job
help me make decisions for my future.

* * * * * * *

I accept What Is. I maintain balance in my mind.
I do not need to assign blame or to accept blame.

* * * * * * *

My belief in myself remains unfaltering.
I maintain good relationships with co-workers.

* * * * * * *

The energy around my work shifts and all is well again.

* * * * * * *

I am open to receiving information that strengthens
my character and helps me to grow.

* * * * * * *

This job is a doorway to opportunity
that enriches my Soul.

Feeling Overwhelmed (commentary)

~~~~~~

Feeling overwhelmed is an indication of ego-identification with the expectations of projects or assignments you have taken on in the physical world. In the case of work, you perceive that the projects or assignments come from a source outside of yourself, that you have "no choice in the matter," or are somehow being the scapegoat or the victim or the fool. What is even more common in the high-pressure workplace is an unconscious acquiescence to the belief that you must appear supremely "busy" and "overwhelmed" in order to fulfill the expectations of being a good worker. Our minds are very easily programmed in this manner because the group consciousness holds the belief that to be important we must run ourselves ragged. This applies to home life too, when you can't let go of the feeling that you haven't done enough for your kids or family. It feels so good to "Get over it!"

Feeling Overwhelmed

The message in this temporary uncomfortable feeling
is revealed to me.

* * * * * *

I separate myself from the group belief that we will
be rewarded for being or appearing overworked.

* * * * * *

All projects that come to me are easily managed
through my skill and talent.

* * * * * *

I know in my heart if it is time for me to create
a new job situation.

Too Much to Do and Too Little Time

The relative importance of the various tasks before me
reveals itself.

* * * * * *

I function with economy of effort.

* * * * * *

Following my inner direction, I take steps
that yield results.

* * * * * *

Tasks that do not call for my immediate attention
miraculously take care of themselves, are rethought,
or are eliminated.

Boredom, Disinterest, or Disconnect

I allow the message of this feeling to be revealed,
so that I may create desired changes.

* * * * * *

My enthusiasm comes from within me
and not from outside circumstances.

* * * * * *

I NOW experience more enjoyment and
enthusiasm in my work.

* * * * * *

I have stimulating interactions with people at work.

* * * * * *

I am grateful to my work for sustaining my life and giving
me a laboratory in which to explore Who I Am.

Boredom or disconnect points to a condition where you are in resistance to your circumstances; where your experience falls short of the highest idea you hold for yourself. It may be time to create something new; or to create a way to have more enjoyment within the existing work environment.

Disharmonious Relationship with a Co-Worker/Colleague

I set aside my personal sensitivities and choose the path of neutrality rather than offense.

* * * * * * *

The nature or purpose of my life intersecting with that of [name] is revealed to me.

* * * * * * *

Opportunities arise to allow healing of this tension between us.

* * * * * * *

I am guided to respond to and interact with [name] in a way that promotes understanding and acceptance.

* * * * * * *

I hold that [name] wishes the best for me, as I wish the best for him/her.

* * * * * * *

I allow [name] to develop some influence, as my own Power is unassailable.

* * * * * * *

By allowing [name] to strive to be my equal, I affirm the strength of my personal power.

Most conflicts in the workplace have to do with a perceived battle for power or influence. These statements reinforce approaches that focus attention on our inner domain and restore peace with quiet strength.

Feeling Unappreciated for Your Talents

I excel at my work because it pleases me,
not to get recognition.

* * * * * *

This unsatisfying experience (or feeling) is temporary and
does not define Who I Am.

* * * * * *

My connection with Who I Am remains constant,
beyond the thoughts or opinions of others.

* * * * * *

This place (environment) in which I find myself
is temporary, like a railway station in the pathway
of my Eternal Life.

* * * * * *

I NOW create a situation where my talents
are freely expressed and valued.

The desire for free and creative self-expression is a basic human need. Feelings of not being appreciated may signal that you are ready for change and growth. Through the message of contrast, you can envision and create a new circumstance where your gifts and talents are appreciated. Dissatisfaction is the stimulation you need to bring about a desired change.[1]

---

[1]Hicks, Esther. *Ask and It Is Given.*

Criticism from Supervisor of Colleague (commentary)

~~~~~~

Giving feedback to another person in a way that invigorates and empowers them is a talent that is expressed naturally by only a few. For most people, it must be taught and modeled and practiced. The way in which we have been trained to use language predisposes us to assign wrong and blame.[1] This tendency to blame is even more likely when a colleague is preoccupied or having a bad day, which is unintentionally projected onto others. Such situations are ideal for practicing forgiveness. At the same time, you must allow for the possibility that the feedback provides critical information for your growth.

---

[1]Rosenberg, Marshall. *Nonviolent Communication.*

Criticism from Supervisor or Colleague

The instruction coming from [supervisor] is intended
to help me thrive in this environment.

* * * * * *

Handling this situation gracefully prepares me
for similar situations in the future.

* * * * * *

Learning to be better in my job makes me better
in other arenas of my life.

* * * * * *

Criticism from my [colleague] is a reflection of
what is going on for him or her, and does not
have to do with me.

* * * * * *

I accept that [colleague or supervisor] may not have
expressed himself/herself in the way he intended.

* * * * * *

I am responsible for my reaction if I take offense,
or feel resistance.

* * * * * *

I accept the learning that is there for me and let it go.

Needing to Have a Serious Talk with Someone

I accept the responsibility to help [name] grow
in his life.

* * * * * * *

I know that I will find the way and the words
to provide feedback in a loving way.

* * * * * * *

I know that my expressing my Truth will benefit [name].

Tense or Intense Situation

Words and action that calm this situation
are revealed to me.

* * * * * * *

[Persons involved] draw energy of calmness and clarity to
forge a constructive solution to our differences.

* * * * * * *

I express my Truth with confidence, at the same time
being open to receiving information
I need for my growth.

*To heal the planet, we learn to communicate our needs in a way that does
not make the other person(s) wrong. Then all can grow.*

Communicating With Those in Charge

I am filled with courage and clarity of mind regarding my
need to communicate to [manager, supervisor etc.] about
the issue or recommendation.

* * * * * *

The right time, right place and right way
to approach [person] open up for me.

* * * * * *

I express my own [the organization's] needs in a way that
does not demand or manipulate or blame.

* * * * * *

[Person] is open to receiving the information
or suggestion I have to offer.

* * * * * *

My communication creates a deeper partnership
between [person] and myself.

*You must be pure-hearted and courageous to convey the truth in situations
of unequal power. When your compatriots turn to you and say "You're
the only one who could say that to her," you know you have been called to
service of the greater good. You formulate your message, and then employ
your inner vision to imagine how the interaction will happen. You invite
guidance, remaining open until there is no more uncomfortable energy
around your vision. Then you take action.*

Workaholic — Creating Better Balance

I receive the message that is in my need or choice to be
consumed by my work.

* * * * * *

I can choose to change my habits at any time.

* * * * * *

I NOW choose to create better balance in my life.

* * * * * *

My work takes its appropriate place amongst
the many things that I enjoy.

* * * * * *

New possibilities for enjoyment other than my work
present themselves to me in unexpected ways.

* * * * * *

The reward I receive from enjoying new activities
equals the joy I receive from my work.

* * * * * *

My self-worth does not come from my activities
or accomplishments.

---

*Extreme devotion to work may be motivated by lust for money, or power,
or to define who you think you are. Filling your every waking moment
with work or activities assures you of your importance. When you stop
and reflect inside yourself, you become aware of the emptiness of these
pursuits. Here, you begin to shift your mind from obsession and anxiety
to a state of openness for growth or change.*

Wanting more Time with Family

I NOW create more work/life balance.

* * * * * * *

The expectations of my work are accomplished easily.

* * * * * * *

New opportunities for enjoying my family arise that are not in conflict with the responsibilities of work.

* * * * * * *

My relationships with family members increase in depth and take on new meaning.

These statements set a new intention. Results follow!

Finding Courage to Change Your Job

Changes in my life are happening to align me
with a new and better way of being in the world.

* * * * * * *

I accept that what is occurring is for my highest good,
even if I do not understand it.

* * * * * * *

What has happened in the past or happened to others
has no bearing on what is happening for me right now.

* * * * * * *

I know that my needs and those of my family are
always met with more abundance than we can imagine.

* * * * * * *

I envision myself moving into the situation/feeling
I have dreamed about in my heart.

* * * * * * *

I embrace *What Is* with courage and fascination.

When the time comes for transition of a job or relationship, it is as if you are swept away in a current of inevitability that is at the same time exhilarating and terrifying. Troubled thoughts arise from old voices in your head retelling fear stories from the past, as well as from reactions of family or so-called friends. You let go of your need for control and ride this wave, trusting your life and your ability to draw to you what allows you to thrive.

Starting a New Job

I am centered, aware, and attuned to the nuances
of this new place/new role that will channel
Joy and Abundance to me.

* * * * * * *

Key people are brought to my awareness
at an opportune time.

* * * * * * *

I behave with extra respect and caution as I explore
the interaction of my energy with the energies
of this new environment.

* * * * * * *

I get extra rest as I process the new events.

* * * * * * *

I give extra attention to myself
as I renew my strength and focus every day.

CHAPTER TEN

LIVING IN GRATITUDE

*Send Gratitude Through Your Body: Bring to mind
something in your life about which you can feel thankful.
Gratitude is among the most profound spiritual healers.
Send this feeling of gratitude through your body. Say thank
you to your heart, your lungs, your kidneys, all your organs.
Thank your legs for walking you. Make it a practice to focus
several times each day on feelings of gratitude.*

Donna Eden, *Energy Medicine*

*Gratitude is a key spiritual courtesy, no less important and
beneficial than showing gratitude and courtesy to others in our
everyday lives. It is appreciated by the soul world no less than it
is by your fellow human beings.*

Zhi Gang Sha, *Soul, Mind, Body Medicine*

Interlude

The Power of Appreciation

When you decide to live in ever-present connection with the *Source of All That Is*, from which you came and of which everything and everyone is a part, Gratitude will be your predominant state of mind. For the time being, the practice of Gratitude opens your heart and grounds you in the NOW. Reflection on what you are grateful for may be included as part of your daily meditation or time of reflection, spoken as a prayer, or periodically used as the focus for an activity in which you write down everything you can think of for which you are grateful.

When disturbing thoughts attack your mind, stemming from judgment of experiences in the past or imagined in the future, gratitude is a practice that soothes and centers. Gratitude reminds you why you are here, and reconnects you with the purpose for which you came.

Every set of affirmations in this book would be well concluded with the Gratitude statements, "And So It Is. Thank You God." Through these statements, you express your certainty that the desires of your heart are known and granted by the *Infinite Good* even before you can voice them. Gratitude creates a highly charged form of mental energy that travels as a wave into the *Field of Pure Potentiality*, where it attaches to and attracts like energy to be drawn to you. Gratitude is a way of expressing your appreciation of the *Universal Mind*, sending a message of what it is you would like to have more of in your life.

You express gratitude for that which exists in tangible form in your life, as well as that which you are waiting to receive. Gratitude sends a big *Yes!* to life. The message of Gratitude is to open you up, saying yes, Lord, give me more and more! More abundance, more prosperity! I can handle it! I deserve it! This state of receptivity is also referred to as *Havingness*. This means the "ability to have" or "allowing yourself to have" or "accepting your abundance and prosperity." Simply put, if you do not believe you deserve it, you will not be able to have it.

This chapter includes examples of Gratitude statements and blessings for mealtime and bedtime, as well as a blessing to sanctify marriage or partnership. Commentary is not provided, as these statements are, for the most part, self-explanatory. Giving thanks for the good things draws more good into our life experience.

An Attitude of Gratitude

I am so grateful as I awaken to another day
of play in this body.

* * * * * * *

I look with appreciation
on everything I see and everyone I meet.

* * * * * * *

My heart opens in wonder at the beauty of Creation and
the kindness of God's children.

* * * * * * *

I am grateful for my family and friends, for laughter and
smiles, for physical comfort, for my life and my dreams,
for the delight of living in this body.

For Comforts of Life

Thank you, Divine Grace, for abundantly meeting
every need of my physical comfort.

* * * * * * *

Every aspect of my care and comfort is assured,
for ever and in all ways.

* * * * * * *

For this I am very grateful, thank you God.

For Energy and Vitality

I move through life with energy and vitality
as is my birthright.

* * * * * * *

My joints move easily. Fluidity pervades
every cell of my body.

* * * * * * *

I am very grateful, thank you God.

Blessing at Mealtime

This meal is imbued with light and harmony, giving
sustenance to our bodies, minds, and souls.

* * * * * * *

May God's Love be taken into our bodies as we consume
this lovely repast.

* * * * * * *

We are very grateful, thank you God.

Blessing and Thanksgiving for Food*

Thank you, dear Heavenly Father-Mother God
for this most wonderful feast of joy.
May all this food turn to health and beauty, love,
Light, joy, peace and harmony.
May it fill our Beings with the Golden Liquid
Light of the Universe,
filling us full of vitality, regeneration, rejuvenation,
immortality consciousness, blessings on our work
and play... more love, more Light,
more joy, more Oneness with All That Is.
Thank you, God

*printed by permission of Bob Dinga and Diana Rose

For Loving Partnership

Thank you, God, for this partner who loves to listen and
share my experiences, just as I revel in listening
and sharing his experiences.

* * * * * * *

Thank you God for opening us to see beyond ourselves.

Blessing for Marriage

Our sacred agreement stimulates the unfolding of
new dimensions of life's purpose.

* * * * * * *

We bask in the wonder of soulful companionship.

* * * * * * *

In one another's supportive presence, we navigate the
challenges of life with strength and resourcefulness.

* * * * * * *

Our partnership stimulates the flowering
of our individual talents and joys.

* * * * * * *

Our relationship is blessed with nurturing friends
and companions.

* * * * * * *

Together in this holy bond, we contribute more fully
to the world.

* * * * * * *

The energies of our lives blend into harmony and oneness
through the Grace of *God*.

* * * * * * *

The earth is brought closer to heaven through our love.

For Family and Friends

Thank you, *God*, for family and friends with whom I am
able to give and receive Love.

* * * * * *

I am grateful for the many ways in which my life is enriched
through the love of family and friends.
Thank You for:

[make a list or speak what comes to mind]

For Meaningful Work

I see and appreciate the ways in which the work I do
touches the lives others. I am so grateful, thank you *God*.

* * * * * * *

I am grateful for the many ways in which the work I do
contributes to people's lives:

[make a list or speak what comes to mind]

For Accomplishments

Thank you, *God*, for my many accomplishments:

[make a list or speak what comes to mind]

For a Balanced Mind

Thank you, God, that I know when to rest and
when to take action, when to get involved
and when to remain separate.

* * * * * * *

Thank you God for the centeredness I experience today.

For Rest and Nurturing

I embrace times of rest and quiet as opportunities
to deepen my experience of the *Divine Light*
that lives within me.

* * * * * * *

Thank you, *God*, for this time of rest and nurturing.

Blessing at Bedtime

Thank you, *God*, for the wonders of this day.

* * * * * * *

I now let go of all thoughts and sink into my bed as I drift
into deep and restful sleep.

* * * * * * *

In sleep, my mind finds comfort in the place of Eternal
Oneness, and all the cells of my body are rejuvenated.

* * * * * * *

I awaken refreshed and ready for a new day of Joy.

For the Beauty of Nature

Thank you, *God*, for the incredible beauty, tranquility, and abundance of Nature that surrounds us.

* * * * * * *

Thank you, *God*, for clean air, clean water, the enjoyment of birds and fish.

* * * * * * *

Thank you, *God*, for new ways to live with Nature without destroying that which gives us Joy and Hope.

CHAPTER ELEVEN

EMBRACING YOUR PATH

The decisions we make today, individually and collectively, will determine whether the planet goes to Hell or goes to Heaven. One thing, however, is sure: we are the transitional generation. The critical choices lie in our hands. Future generations will know who we were. They will think of us often. They will curse us, or they will bless us.

Marianne Williamson, *A Return to Love*

Interlude

We Are the Ones We've Been Waiting For

Everywhere the grand wakeup call is going out. Messages are coming to you in your dreams; a caption in a highway roadsign takes on sudden new meaning; you receive an instantaneous response to a request that flitted across your mind; hope becomes the campaign slogan of a presidential hopeful.

Through the offerings of the incredible teachers speaking in our world today, we have come to know it is time to step up to what it is we came to do:

> *There is a holy return in the air today, despite the pain, despite the conflicts, enough people have taken on its mandate, consciously or unconsciously, to have already caused the feeling of a cautious excitement, a hope for Heaven.[1]*

It is time to begin playing fully in our game. Oh, we've been around the block a few times, thousands of lifetimes, some say — long enough to have acquired a fabricated identity that masquerades as our real self, acting out role after role in a world of illusion. But we are seeing through that now. It is the depth of these experiences — our forays into darkness — that empower us to choose a new way of Being.

We find ourselves needing to remember who we really are so that we might have a new idea, a new belief about what is real. We are waking up to our ability to create our lives from the inside out. We have reached the point where there is no roadmap. We have signed on to the incredible journey as we embrace the ultimate paradox, an experience at the same time deeply personal and universal.

We start from where we are. We don't have to join a religious group, follow a guru, travel to a distant land, because what we seek is now coming to us. Doing any or all those things is fine too, but we see that the truth is bigger than any one thing or idea. The veils of secrecy have been lifted. What has been held in proprietary custody for thousands of years in order to protect its sanctity is flowing into the hands of guardians and emissaries of the truth. Who are these guardians and emissaries of the truth? *We* are.

A few tenets for the journey:

We open to everything but attach to nothing.

We behold the Divine Light of Immortal Spirit shining through each person.

We forgive everyone, including ourselves, in every circumstance.

We focus our thoughts on that which increases our vibrational frequency.

We allow our personal world to be recreated as a world of peace and harmony.

We become new people (we are literally born again) as we are unburdened of the pain aspects of ourselves.

We begin exploring what it really means that there is only ONE of us here.

We foster the connection to Love and Light in the young people.

We start where we are, and we end up Home.

---

[1] Williamson, Marianne. *A Return to Love.*

Creating a New Idea of Work

My work is my ministry.

* * * * * * *

I NOW create a new avenue of expression
through which to extend Love.

* * * * * * *

I understand my real work
is to minister to human hearts.

* * * * * * *

My contribution to life expands as I am able to receive it.

* * * * * * *

The Universe abundantly supports me as I create
new ways to support others.

* * * * * * *

I NOW take my next step to becoming
the best I am capable of being.

Manifesting What You Desire (commentary)

~~~~~~

This is the Five Part "Prayer Treatment" as taught in Religious Science.[1]
Steps one and two affirm that All is governed by a supreme and benevolent
Force, identifying oneself to be within that umbrella of Love. The request
is then stated in step three, followed by statements of release and gratitude.
This is a powerful practice when done with a partner, or may be offered
on behalf of another person. Results or "demonstrations" come when you
state your own desires because you are more likely to be ready to receive
what you are asking for. If you are not truly ready, your prayer may bring
you face to face with an old idea you need to clear or a situation for growth.

---

[1] Holmes, Ernest. *The Science of Mind.*

Manifesting What You Desire

Everything in the Universe is governed by the *Supreme
Love of All That Is.*
[or *Divine Love; Source Energy; God*]

* * * * * * *

I know that I am also governed by this same *Love.*

* * * * * * *

A new [love partnership; job; home; car; roommate; pair of
shoes — whatever!] is brought to me in the right way
at the right and perfect time.

* * * * * * *

I now release this into the Universe of Love, knowing that
It Is Already So.
[Visualize a ball of light containing the desired object and
float it off into the cosmos]

* * * * * * *

Thank you, God.

Receiving Guidance While You Sleep
(commentary)

~~~~~~~~~~~~~~~~~~~~~~~~~~~~~~~~~~

It is a common practice for many people who are not religious or devout to teach their children to say a prayer before going to sleep.

We often suggest that someone "sleep on it" when they are in a state of confusion or distress. Most people can relate a story of an idea or solution that was present in their minds miraculously upon waking.

While much about sleep remains a mystery to science, most people accept that sleep transports us to a domain where forces other than those we have placed in charge of the waking world are in action. In the domain of sleep, the controlling egoic mind steps aside and frees our subconscious mind to connect into "the field of pure potentiality" where the thoughts we are offering attract an energetic response that is in accord with what we are seeking.

In our waking life, many of us are addicted to the struggle and the stimulation that comes from conquering a problem through the force of our will and effort. The other world of sleep is a good testing ground for our blossoming affirmation skills because our ego isn't around to interfere or confuse us.

Try writing down a statement of the thing you are desiring, speak it out loud, then place the paper near your bed or under your pillow as you sleep. Upon waking, you will know that energy has been put in motion around the request you have made.

Receiving Guidance While You Sleep

Clarity on… [see examples below] …is brought to this
question/situation as I rest my body and mind in sleep.

I awaken refreshed and certain.
Thank you for this gift.

~~~~~~~~~~~~~~~~~~~~~~~~~~~~~~~~~~

State the problem, for example:
…solving the unpleasant relationship between me and my coworker;
…deciding whether or not to accept leadership of our Homeowner's
Association;
…figuring out the best way to present my findings at next week's meeting;
…how to respond to my son's decision to quit school;
…designing a more effective layout for my website…
and allow the ideas to flow into your mind during sleep.

Creating Change

I accept and embrace God's timing as right and perfect.

* * * * * * *

Everything needed to create my Change
is already in motion.

* * * * * * *

I can see, feel, smell, taste my new situation.

* * * * * * *

I walk in the NOW with Patience and Grace.
I do what must be done.

* * * * * * *

I bless circumstances for supporting me as I open myself to
receive more of my Good.

Change is a time of letting go, of breaking down, which fills us with uncertainty. Change is painful for us as long as we define ourselves to be at the effect of forces beyond our control (to be victims) rather than to own our position as creators mapping our destiny. The positive aspect of change is that it throws us back to discovering and relying on our deepest resources. Desperation opens us to hearing our inner voice. This set of affirmations sets up an energy for change to move forward, and for us to gracefully embrace our inner wisdom.

Creating a Love Partnership

My Lovemate has enraptured my soul and
will never let it go,
just as I have enraptured his [hers].

* * * * * * *

My Lovemate and I are deeply sensual partners exploring
the unique communication
of *Infinite Love.*

* * * * * * *

My Lovemate walks with me now,
laughing and loving me unceasingly.

This is an example of a vision to create a Love Partnership.
Once you can experience the feeling of partnership within your soul, you
affirm that the person is already beside you, sharing every moment with
you, as you gaze soulfully into one another's eyes.
You continue to refine your vision as the Universe brings you potential
matches until one day Aha! there he (she) is next to you.
In the time until your partner arrives to be at your side, you bask in the
Infinite Love of the Divine.

Having Nurturing Relationships

Our home is a sanctuary that draws like-minded others to
gather and explore intellectually, spiritually,
and artistically.

* * * * * * *

Every person in my life is there through mutual agreement
to nurture and help one another grow.

* * * * * * *

I attract new people into my life who support me
in becoming the person I wish to be.

* * * * * * *

My spirit is a source of strength, wellbeing, and growth to
those who are attracted to seek my company.

* * * * * * *

Those whose purpose in my life is completed take their
leave with proper closure — and I wish them well.

---

*There are people who are draining to have around and there are people
who are sustaining to interact with. All persons in your life are there for
your learning — for a reason, a season, or a lifetime as the saying goes. A
person who drains your energy calls you to explore and clear the thought
that brings you to be subject to them. At the same time, you must be
mindful how you project your own energy so as not to drain or use others
for "venting" rather than working things out yourself. However, when
you are sick or in deep need of help and a kind-hearted angel comes to your
aid, you remember to joyfully accept and just Let Grace Happen.*

Vision for a New Year

May we be filled with gratitude to be alive
in this amazing time.

* * * * * *

May we flow into partnership with the *Infinite Source*.

* * * * * *

May we find new ways to contribute
to an expansion of Greater Consciousness in our world.

* * * * * *

May we allow our energy vibration to accelerate
as our channels of higher Wisdom open.

* * * * * *

May we embrace change as our old ways
of orienting to the world disappear.

* * * * * *

May we have courage to stand strong amidst
the swirling chaos of that which is passing away.

* * * * * *

May we be confident and Know that All is Well
in our inner Being.

* * * * * *

May we live to see the Transformation of the planet into a
place of Love where our young ones will play.

* * * * * *

May we see the flowering of the Purpose
for which we were born.

Cultivating an Attitude of Openness and Anticipation

My heart is open to know and express
the glory of *Divine Spirit* in this moment,
and in my vision of the future.

* * * * * *

I have faith that there is a higher purpose unfolding
within the unknown and unseen in my Life.

* * * * * *

My horizons are filled with hope and eagerness
for all experiences my Life brings to me.

* * * * * *

My life is unfolding with blessings far above and beyond
anything I have ever envisioned for myself.

Vision for a New Way of Being in the World

Interesting, talented, unique, and wonderful individuals
are drawn into my world to play with me.

* * * * * * *

I embrace the direction my life is going
and what it brings to me.
I give up trying to orchestrate how things will happen.

* * * * * * *

I allow myself to experience Happiness.
Never have I been so happy nor so blessed.

* * * * * * *

New dimensions of my Self are revealed in each interaction
within my personal community.

* * * * * * *

I give out healing in every way natural to me,
and I am healed over and over again by others.

---

*This is a personal vision statement written to affirm and encourage the
unfolding of my own life path. It could have included other things, such as
abundant flowering of my writing. You are invited to construct your own
vision using some of these statements if they resonate with you, adding those
of your own creation. You may find fulfillment in creating and offering
similar statements in support of your loved ones.*

Staying on the Path

I open myself to Light.
Every day I grow in understanding of my Divine Nature.

* * * * * * *

I relinquish fear and learn to Allow and Trust.
I Know that *Love* IS.

* * * * * * *

I tenaciously pursue the keys to Understanding,
which are within my grasp.

* * * * * * *

Every day I see more clearly that NOW is the only existence.
There is no other place to go, nowhere else to be
in the future. I am already HERE.

* * * * * * *

Light pours throughout every cell of my Being, absorbing
and radiating back to the Universe.

* * * * * * *

In this moment I respond to perfect instructions
on a cellular, mind, and spirit level.

* * * * * * *

I humbly offer my desire to contribute to Life in accordance
with the purpose for which I came.

Blessed be!

REFERENCES

Allen, Richard. (2001). *Getting Things Done: The Art of Stress-Free Productivity*. New York: Penguin Books.

Cady, H. Emilie. (1903; 2003). *Lessons in Truth*. Unity Village, Missouri.

Chopra, Deepak. (2004). *The Book of Secrets: Unlocking the Hidden Dimensions of Your Life*. New York: Three Rivers Press.

Chopra, Deepak. (1993). *Ageless Body, Timeless Mind: The Quantum Alternative to Growing Old*. New York: Three Rivers Press.

Chopra, Deepak. (1994). *The Seven Spiritual Laws of Success: A Practical Guide to the Fulfillment of Your Dreams*. San Rafael, California: Amber-Allen / New World Library.

Dyer, Wayne. (1989). *You'll See It When You Believe It: The Way to Your Personal Transformation*. New York: William Morrow and Company, Inc.

Dyer, Wayne. (2004). *The Power of Intention: Learning to Co-Create Your World Your Way*. Carlsbad, California: Hay House.

Dyer, Wayne. (2006). (CD) *Being in Balance: 9 Principles for Creating Habits to Match Your Desires*. Carlsbad, California: Hay House.

Eden, Donna. (1998). *Energy Medicine*. New York: Tarcher/ Putnam.

Foundation for Inner Peace. (1975; 1985). *A Course in Miracles.* Tiburon, California: Foundation for Inner Peace.

Fumia, Molly. (2003). *Safe Passage: Words to Help the Grieving.* York Beach, ME: Conari Press.

Gibran, Kahlil. (1962). *The Prophet.* New York: Alfred A. Knopf.

Gray, John, PhD. (1992). *Men Are From Mars, Women Are From Venus: A Practical Guide for Improving Communication and Getting What You Want in Your Relationships.* New York: HarperCollins.

Hawkins, David R. (2002). *Power Vs. Force: The Hidden Determinants of Human Behavior.* Carlsbad, CA: Hay House.

Hay, Louise L. (1984). *You Can Heal Your Life.* Santa Monica, CA: Hay House.

Hicks, Esther and Jerry Hicks (The Teachings of Abraham). (2004). *Ask and It Is Given: Learning to Manifest Your Desires.* Carlsbad, CA: Hay House.

Hicks, Esther and Jerry Hicks (The Teachings of Abraham). (2006). *The Amazing Power of Deliberate Intent: Living the Art of Allowing.* Carlsbad, CA: Hay House.

Holmes, Ernest. (1938; 1998). *The Science of Mind: A Philosophy, a Faith, a Way of Life.* New York: Tarcher/Putnam.

Kasl, Charlotte. (2001). *If the Buddha Married: Creating Enduring Relationships on a Spiritual Path.* New York: Penguin.

Katie, Byron. (2002). *Loving What Is: Four Questions That Can Change Your Life.* New York: Three Rivers Press.

Lipton, Bruce. (2005). *The Biology of Belief: Unleashing the Power of Consciousness, Matter and Miracles.* Santa Rosa, California: Mountain of Love/Elite Books.

McCartney, Francesca. (2005). *Body of Health: The New Science of Intuition Medicine for Energy & Balance.* Novato, California: Nataraj/New World Library.

McTaggart, Lynn. (2002). *The Field: The Quest for the Secret Force of the Universe.* New York: HarperCollins.

Morrissey, Mary Manin (Editor). (2002). *New Thought: A Practical Spirituality.* New York: Tarcher/Putnam.

Myss, Caroline. (1996). *The Anatomy of Spirit: The Seven Stages of Power and Healing.* New York: Three Rivers Press.

Myss, Caroline. (1997). *Why People Don't Heal, and How they Can.* New York: Three Rivers Press.

O'Donohue, John. (1998). *Anam Cara: A Book of Celtic Wisdom.* New York: HarperCollins.

Rosenberg, Marshall B., PhD and Arun Gandhi. (2003). *Nonviolent Communication: A Language of Life.* New York: PuddleDancer.

Sha, Zhi Gang. (2002). *Power Healing: The Four Keys to Energizing Your Body, Mind & Spirit.* San Francisco: Harper.

Sha, Zhi Gang. (2006). *Soul Mind Body Medicine: A Complete Soul Healing System for Optimum Health and Vitality.* Novato, California: New World Library.

Tolle, Eckhart. (2005). *A New Earth: Awakening to Your Life's Purpose.* New York: Plume/Penguin.

Walsch, Neale Donald. (1996). *Conversations With God: An Uncommon Dialogue (book 1).* New York: Putnam.

Van Praagh, James. (2000). *Healing Grief: Reclaiming Life After Any Loss.* New York: New American Library

Williamson, Marianne. (1994). *Illuminata: A Return to Prayer.* New York: Riverhead Books.

Williamson, Marianne. (1975). *A Return to Love: Reflections on the Principles of A Course In Miracles.* New York: Harper Collins.

Yogananda, Paramahansa. (1988). *Where There Is Light: Insight and Inspiration for Meeting Life's Challenges.* Los Angeles, CA: Self-Realization Fellowship.

Starting From Where You Are

In the last century, a host of scientific rationalist thinkers of our country, recognizing the aversion of the general public to any reference to a *Supreme Being*, produced an outpouring of applications of fundamental *New Thought* principles into broadening arenas of nontraditional psychology including hypnosis, Neurolinguistic Programming, EFT (Emotional Freedom Technique) and other new healing modalities collectively relegated to the *self-help* genre.

More recently, we have entered a new era in which the general public is embracing more and more the idea that our expectations are determining factors in our experience, as supported by the exciting research into Quantum Physics. The popularity of the film *What the Bleep Do We Know*, followed by overnight success of the film *The Secret* indicate a new level of awakening of these ideas in the mass consciousness. How nice it would be if we could simply write what we want on a piece of paper and have it instantly come true!

Nonetheless, every person who devotes even minimal practice to these principles can begin to demonstrate for him or herself the myriad ways in which thoughts (beliefs) determine one's experience and enjoyment of the world. This realization is at once the greatest and most frightening news possible. How empowering it is to realize that our beliefs are the causative factor in how our life unfolds! But how dare you say that the grumpy people I encounter in the grocery store are a mirror of my inner state! What about those dark secret thoughts I get a glimpse of floating in the murky depths of my mind? What is it I believe, anyway?

The wisest teachers of today advise us to dis-identify from our thoughts, forgive ourselves and others, maintain a positive outlook no matter what happens — yet this is so much easier said than done. Even after we participate in a workshop, or receive treatment through one of the psychological approaches, we so quickly revert to our previously established mental patterns. The more we learn about the working of our mind and the depth of the false egoic selves we have allowed to rule our consciousness, the more humble we become as we realize the vastness of the challenge. It becomes easier to forgive others as we work through the layers of unconsciousness that arise in our own thoughts. We are called to become vigilant in every moment. Slowly, we become more awake, more aware, more the observer watching our thoughts.

If the outer world we see is the mirror of our inner state, then the mundane experiences and situations of daily life provide an ideal laboratory for our learning. We can sit in church on Sundays, and attend workshop after workshop, but our deepest learning often arises out of what comes up for us in relation to other persons or to particular circumstances we encounter at those gatherings.

Go inside and discover your Truth, and the Truth will set you free.

ANNIE ELIZABETH'S STORY

Since early childhood, I have been a student of the human mind in relation to the Great Mystery of the Self, explorations of the Soul, and why we are here. I was intensely devoted to the Christian religion in my youth, but the teachings of the church soon failed to support me in my deepening spiritual quest. As time went on, I explored Buddhist thought and practices, delving into other Eastern meditation and healing traditions in my college years as did many of my generation. In my early thirties, I spent four years living and working in Asia, where I experienced two very different Buddhism-based social structures — in Sri Lanka and then in Japan — each with their unique healing practices.

Following my return to the USA, I engaged in a training program that provided me with skills in "grounding and running energy," aura cleansing, directing universal life force energy to heal the body. We practiced conducting intuitive "aura readings" and "healings." A key tenet of this training was that all persons are "psychic," and all of us "read energy;" but most of us are not aware that we have these abilities. Basic skills acquired during this training included an awareness of one's own "space" or energy field (aura), an understanding of how one's energy field interacts with that of other persons, and an ability to "see" pictures in the mind (as if on a movie screen in the center of the head, behind the eyes).

At an early age, I knew that the underpinnings of Western allopathic medicine — with a chemical and pharmaceutical approach as its basis — were not compatible with my deepest understanding of health and disease. My father was a surgeon, his father was also a physician, and it was instilled in me at an early age that there was no higher calling in this life than to be a practitioner of medicine. Today my brother is also a surgeon, and my sister is a nurse who is married to a surgeon. It was natural to me to design my career around the education of future doctors, to which I devoted myself at Stanford University School of Medicine for 19 years, retiring in 2008 as Assistant Dean for Medical Education.

During the time of my career in the School of Medicine, I continued my study of the human mind, expanding my longstanding interest in Eastern and healing modalities such as acupuncture and the Ayurvedic medicine I experienced in Sri Lanka. In these years, I met chiropractors who employed "muscle testing" as a diagnostic tool, and explored the new science of *Energy Medicine* or *Intuition Medicine*.

In the environment of the medical center, I witnessed all manner of medical illness and the rare successes — but more often staggering failures — of the medical industry to *cure* or in many cases even satisfactorily *treat* disease. My explorations into the work of holistic physicians deepened my conviction that the mind — our attitudes, thoughts, and beliefs — plays a fundamental role in illness and healing that is overlooked and even subjugated in the practice of allopathic medicine. (This is changing quite rapidly as we are experiencing a quantum leap forward in human consciousness and mind/body medicine even as I write this.)

In conjunction with these explorations, about six years ago, I was attracted to a body of metaphysical literature and practices loosely attached to a philosophy known as *New Thought*, including the channeled tome *A Course in Miracles*. A key tenet underlying these writings is the search for a deeper understanding of what the Christ and other great mystics came to teach us. Among the key messages are that *discovering God is a process; the truth of God is found by searching within ourselves; our life experience is determined by our beliefs* — which are quite opposite of the constrictive teaching we received from most religions and our childhood teachers.

A second key tenet of *A Course in Miracles* is that freeing our minds is dependent upon our *engaging with others*. All thought is energy, all minds are connected, and we free ourselves through teaching (being a living example for) others, as we honor all others as our teachers. My connection with my "spiritual family" at Unity and Religious Science churches gave me the greatest *aha!* experiences of my lifetime. You may be leery of groups of any kind, and for good reason. You may be tired of the dogma of your own church. I encourage you to seek out a New Thought church in your area, join a group studying *A Course in Miracles*, or gather folks together for a discussion group at your home.

As to the origin of my writing, since my youth I have been captivated by the intimacy of the written word and have documented the stages of my life's learning through poetry and journaling. Several years before my sojourn into *New Thought*, I developed the ability to connect with a "higher voice" that would speak to me inside my head, and with which (it always referred to itself as "we") I could conduct lively conversations. This was a miraculous phenomenon for me, but one which I knew in the context of the day-to-day world raised serious concerns about my sanity. So I quietly guarded these exchanges and shared about it with very few people.

At some time during this period of expansion to *New Thought*, I had the wonderful experience of reading *Conversations with God*. Communion with the writings in that series of books gave me solace and encouragement to embrace my own "conversations" as a precious gift of insight. In recent years, I began creating statements of healing intention to support friends and family members experiencing life's inimitable challenges. Such offerings became so routine in our household that one day my son said, "You should put these into a book!" and that was the beginning of *Affirmations for Everyday Living*.

Certain scenarios included in the book clearly arose out of my own life experience, while others are quite divergent from my particular circumstances. The process of writing a particular affirmation necessitated that I place my consciousness into the scenario, whether pursuing bliss or immersed in trouble, then opening to receive statements to address or reverse the situation. I experienced resistance within myself to certain scenarios, necessitating some inner work over a period of days to open to the message that was waiting to come through. Somewhere in the process, I naturally began enriching some sets of statements with personal commentary, sharing an anecdote or providing references for the ideas underpinning the affirmations.

This book is offered from my heart as an instrument for your personal healing of mind, body, and soul, with the hope that it stimulates you to contribute your own talent and insight to the incredible planetary awakening.

More books from River Sanctuary Publishing...

The Unorthodox Life: Walking Your Own Path to the Divine, by Kathy McCall, 2009. $15.95

Notes to Self: Meditations on Being, by Christy Deena, 2011. $15.95

A Space Between: Adventures and Lessons Between Lives, by Ardeth DeVries, 2010. $13.95

How Alternation Can Change Your Life: Finding the Rhythms of Health and Happiness, by Andrew Oser, 2010. $15.95

American Maze, a novel by Ralph Peduto, 2010. $14.95

Illuminating the Mundane: Transformational Silk Painting and Haiku, (full color) by Billie Furuichi, 2010. $18.95

Available from:

www.spiritualpathfinder.com

River Sanctuary Publishing
P.O. Box 1561
Felton, California 95018
www.riversanctuarypublishing.com

We offer custom book design and production with worldwide availability through print-on-demand, with the best author-friendly terms in the industry. Specializing in inspirational, spiritual and self-help books, biography, and memoirs.